"Candice is like the ghost whisperer of millennial dating. Whether you're just starting to put yourself out there or your heart's been broken too many times to count, she'll meet you exactly where you're at—judgment free!"

—**Iman Hariri-Kia, sex and relationships editor at Bustle**

"Dating books of the past twenty years will tell you that you can trick someone into loving you by playing games, and knowing the exact minute to second ratio for text backs. Jalili busts this notion out of the water with her acknowledging the real anxiety behind dating and how you are getting in your own way. Her humor, knowledge, and lived experience helps the women of 2020 to use our voices, know ourselves, and just send the text. When Jalili talks about 'Eunice,' she's speaking about all of our inner anxious dependent voices, the one we feel shame and embarrassment about. Her humor and lived experiences allow us to look at that part of ourselves with an honest giggle and a breath to take a real look at ourselves and our 'part' in the situation. Excited to share this book with my clients and colleagues!"

—**Emmalee Bierly, LMFT, couples and sex therapist, owner of the West Chester Therapy Group, and co-host of *The Shrink Chicks* podcast**

"*Just Send the Text* is the dating advice book millennial women have been waiting for. Candice Jalili is the only writer who understands the extreme specificities of dating in the modern age, and her advice is fresh, relatable, and downright hilarious. It's impossible to finish *Just Send the Text* without feeling inspired to take the reins on your dating life."

—**Alexia LaFata, editor at *New York* magazine**

"In looking for love, a relationship should enhance your life rather than make you feel less than. Since self-doubt hijacks you from joy, I'm happy Candice Jalili is encouraging people to trust their intuition to ultimately form more fulfilling connections, within and with others."

—Jennifer Taitz, author of *How to be Single and Happy*

"For half a decade, I've loved devouring Candice Jalili's thousands upon thousands of sex and dating articles that span across every relevant byline on the internet. *Just Send the Text* takes Jalili's expert-driven advice and empowering message to a whole different level. In her heartfelt and bitingly real debut book, Jalili inspires a generation of young women to not only release themselves from the shackles of modern-day dating anxiety but to garner freedom and authenticity in *every* aspect of their lives. Make no mistake, *Just Send the Text* isn't just a book about falling in love with another person, its core message lies in learning how to fall in love with *yourself*—in all your messy, beautiful, unique glory. Jalili's whip-smart yet wildly accessible (and refreshingly humorous!) voice carries the key to the most life-enhancing lesson of all: how to get over the fear of rejection and live a life that honors your fabulous, wild, authenticity."

—Zara Barrie, author of *Girl, Stop Passing Out in Your Makeup: The Bad Girl's Guide to Getting Your Sh*t Together*

"As the former sex and relationships editor at *Cosmopolitan*, Elite Daily, and *Women's Health*, I wish I had *Just Send the Text* to give to every reader, podcast listener, and friend who ever asked me for advice. This book has EVERY ANSWER that anyone who's currently dating or in a situationship could possibly need. And, the best part is, Candice delivers it all in her signature hilarious and self-effacing way. She also fact checks every truism with real stories from *real* people, plus cold, hard science (that honestly, even long-term couples should familiarize themselves with). If you've ever had one of those moments where your heart is beating a million times a minute, your face is hot AF, the hairs on your arms are standing up, and your breath is caught in your throat because you have *no* idea what to do next with that person you like, do yourself a huge solid and read this book. I'm not overselling it when I say the lessons in here will change your life. Trust me: I'm a former Eunice, too."

— **Faye Brennan editor-in-chief of *Eat This, Not That!***

"If dating ever makes you anxious, this book is a must-read. Candice *gets* it — and her signature blend of empathy and humor will have you hooked. This book feels like a hug from your wise big sister who's been in your shoes."

— **Hannah Orenstein, author of *Head Over Heels***

"Jalili's *Just Send the Text* is an absolute must-read for any woman battling dating anxiety (hi, all of us!). Each page helps — and encourages the reader in a super cute older sister-y kind of way — let go of the stress that comes with planning dates, initiating the first move, and the dreaded reply time debate. Be prepared to share this book with your group chat because, yup, you *will* feel personally victimized by the advice in here, you *will* think 'Omg, it's me!' every two pages, and you *will* be a better dater because of it. Promise."

— **Taylor Andrews, assistant editor at *Cosmopolitan***

An Expert's Guide to Letting Go of the Stress and Anxiety of Modern Dating

JUST

SEND

THE

TEXT

...

Candice Jalili

TILLER PRESS

New York London Toronto Sydney New Delhi

An Imprint of Simon & Schuster, Inc.
1230 Avenue of the Americas
New York, NY 10020

First Tiller Press trade paperback edition February 2021

TILLER PRESS and colophon are registered
trademarks of Simon & Schuster, Inc.

For information about special discounts for bulk purchases,
please contact Simon & Schuster Special Sales at
1-866-506-1949 or business@simonandschuster.com.

The Simon & Schuster Speakers Bureau can bring authors
to your live event. For more information or to book an
event, contact the Simon & Schuster Speakers Bureau at
1-866-248-3049 or visit our website at www.simonspeakers.com.

Interior design by Lewelin Polanco

Manufactured in the United States of America

1 3 5 7 9 10 8 6 4 2

Library of Congress Cataloging-in-Publication Data
has been applied for.

ISBN 978-1-9821-5478-3
ISBN 978-1-9821-5479-0 (ebook)

To all my fellow Eunices

CONTENTS

WTF Is Just Sending the Text?

L et's set the scene here: It was my sophomore year of college in the early 2010s at Santa Clara University—go, Broncos!—and I was sure that I was in love with a junior boy who was by no means my boyfriend. Let's call him Jack. Jack and I first met when a mutual friend set us up for my sorority's winter formal.

Full disclosure: It was college, it was a sorority date event, and I was drunk, so I don't quite remember every detail of what went down between Jack and me that night. But I'll tell you what I do remember. We met at the most clichéd of college locations: a pre-game in a grimy off-campus apartment that took place before the actual formal. We split a bottle of André at the pregame—again, so college—and he made fun of the saltines I kept in my purse to snack on. At the actual event, we agreed the catered Chinese food was bad and we had a few dance-offs, during which I failed to do the Funky Chicken with my heels on. Oh, and at some point, we made a bet about something I cannot for the life of me remember, but it involved me kissing him at midnight if I lost. At the end of the night, I—shocker—lost whatever bet we made, and we kissed outside my dorm. By this point, I was certain that I had met the love of my life.

I even still remember the first text he ever sent me: "It's Jack. Only use this number if absolutely necessary." It came about five minutes after our good-night kiss. *Swoon!*

I remember lying on my twin XL bed reading that text over and over again, antsy for my roommate Meg to wake up so I could tell her that I was completely and totally in *love*. But more important, I wanted her to wake up so we could get to work on crafting a response. Because for me, at that point in my life, anyway, crushing on someone meant becoming totally and completely overrun with self-doubt. Case in point: In just a few hours after meeting Jack, I had transformed from a (relatively) normal person into an Anxious Hot Mess.

Why did liking Jack turn me into *such* an anxious mess? Because for me at that time, liking him pretty much meant there was no possible way he liked me back. I wholeheartedly believed guys were only interested in beer-drinking, casual-sex-loving, commitment-hating, too-cool-for-texting Chill Girls. If I could morph myself into one of them, maybe I stood a chance. But as far as I was concerned, the idea that I could win him over by just being myself* seemed about as likely as the sky suddenly raining arugula.

Aside from the fact that I was pretty much the antithesis of the Chill Girl described above, accepting that he could just like me exactly as I am was totally impossible for me for two reasons. First, there was the fact that I'd created a stark power imbalance within our relationship† by placing him at the very top of the proverbial totem pole and myself at the very bottom. While I was hyper-critical of pretty much every move I made in his presence, Jack could do absolutely no wrong in my eyes. The moment I decided I liked him, he ascended onto an imaginary pedestal and there was no getting

---

* To be clear, "myself" at the time was a champagne-drinking, just-kissing, commitment-craving, rapid-texting Not Even Slightly Chill Girl.

† Obvs this is a loose term here (lol).

him down from there. He was no longer just the mildly cute guy I'd met at the grimy pregame. He was now *my dream man.* My perfect human. The Noah to my Allie. The Romeo to my Juliet. The Jim to my Pam. You get the picture. I was really into him . . . and trying to just, like, *chill* when you've put that much pressure on getting the approval of one guy you went to one formal with isn't exactly easy.

A huge part of my insecurity boiled down to my own relationship history—or lack thereof. I didn't enter my first real "official" relationship, which also happens to be the one I'm still currently in, until I was 23. In other words, until then, I'd never had things just seamlessly work out with someone I liked. Having things burst into flames—or, more typically, uneventfully fizzle out—was my norm. And I lived in a constant state of fear of having things not work out all over again. As soon as I started to catch even the slightest trace of a feeling, my mind began subconsciously bracing itself for what it believed would be the inevitable end. Why would *Jack*, whom I had superglued so tightly onto a pedestal in my mind, want to date a lame relationship virgin like *me*? Why would he be any different from the other handful of guys who had, for one reason or another, decided they didn't want an "official" relationship with me?

I decided the only way someone like myself could realistically end up with a guy as incredible as Jack was to play every single one of my cards exactly right, until I essentially conned him into a relationship. This meant doing things like choosing to sit in my dorm room twiddling my thumbs instead of going to the game he invited me to because *duh!* I had to play it cool! This also meant immediately taking a screenshot of the now infamous "It's Jack. Only use this number if absolutely necessary" text and every other text he sent me after that and sending them to all of my friends to help me craft the *perfect* response—I don't remember what we wound up going with, but it was probably something super *chill* like "got it." This meant spending hours with my friends discussing what he meant when he said "I guess I kind of like you" after our first sleepover: Was it him telling me he liked me in his own sarcastic way . . . or did he actually just not like me that much?!!? What exactly did "kind of" mean? This meant pretending I knew what 69ing was when I most definitely did not—yes, I'd heard everyone laugh when the number came up in math class, but, like, how did the numbers translate to body parts in real time?!

It was madness. And, surprise of the century, it didn't work out. After months of me acting just straight-up weird around Jack, things eventually fizzled out between us. I moved on to seeing someone I felt much more comfortably lukewarm about, and he moved on to seeing various girls I'd spend hours stalking on social media.

Jack was pretty much completely out of my life until my birthday rolled around that July. I was out with a bunch of friends from home *and* that guy I was lukewarm about when, much to my extremely excited surprise, I got a "happy birthday" Snapchat from Jack. That Snapchat turned into weeks of texting, and the weeks of texting turned into me coming up with an excuse to make the two-hour drive back to school, where he was still staying for the summer. And as much as I told myself that hanging out with him this time would be different, it wasn't. He was still pretty obviously not that into me, and I was still pretty obviously letting his presence turn me into a game-playing anxious mess. Every "cool" move I thought I was making, from hinting at other guys I was seeing to trying way too hard to play my two-hour drive to see him off as NBD, only wound up making things more weird. By the time I left him, I was exhausted.

I wasn't just drained by the *painfully* cringeworthy events of the night, which included but weren't limited to me going in for a kiss and him flipping it into a platonic hug good-bye. I was exhausted by the past six months of trying to make him like me. I was so bent out of shape trying to force myself to do whatever it took to make this person I'd deemed "perfect" like me as much as I liked him that I eventually lost both him and myself in the process. Jack never got the chance to get to know the real me. Even if he really did like the version of myself that I was presenting to him, the person he was falling for would have been an anxiety-ridden, insecure shell.

So, I decided to send him a text. And this time, I didn't share the text with anyone to edit and reframe and proofread. I didn't write eight thousand drafts of it in my notes. Instead, in a stream of consciousness, I just wrote everything I'd been feeling up until that point. I said I really liked him and that I felt sorry because my feelings for him turned me into a weird version of myself that subsequently squashed any chance he would have had to get to know the real me.

. . . And guess what, now we're engaged!

Lol, JK. He didn't respond. Yep, that's right: After months of stressing myself out over this guy, he ghosted me. I put myself out there and was faced with the literal *worst* possible outcome. But, much to my own surprise, I didn't die. Here I am, almost a decade later, alive to tell the tale.

I mean, don't get me wrong. By the second day, when I realized he wasn't responding, I spent about an hour sobbing to my friend Cori as she comforted me on the couch in my mom's living room. And for weeks after, I saw him posting on social media—proof that he was alive and *did* have a phone and he *did* see my text—and it filled me with a seething rage. But after some time, I was just over everything having to do with him. And not because I met someone new to channel my energy into. No, I was able to move forward because—despite what I told myself the entire time I was chasing him—I realized Jack liking me had no real bearing on how I felt about *myself*. Being denied so harshly by someone I spent the past six months fantasizing about having a future with obviously hurt. But it took being rejected by him to remind myself that I still had a great life without him.

To be fair, he did apologize to me for ghosting when we got back to school in the fall. But the funny thing is I didn't even care at that point. When I look back on the entire Jack saga, the only thing I *don't* regret is sending that text. That's the only glimpse of the real me I ever managed to give him. And he rejected it right there on the spot! I wasted *so much time* driving myself insane over a guy whom I was able to get over pretty quickly. I experienced the heartbreak I was so afraid of feeling and . . . I lived. TBH, it was *fine*. I was *fine*. Actually, I was even more than fine. I was better than I'd been over the previous six months. The pressure of trying to be someone I'm not in order to get someone else's approval had suddenly been lifted, and the liberation felt more refreshing to me than cannonballing into an ice-cold pool on a hot summer day.

Jack ghosting me told me everything I needed to know about him and me. I wasted months stressing over someone *who didn't even like me enough to send a reply*. I wasted half a year of my life when I could have, instead, been doing *literally anything else with that time*. All it took was that one text to set me free from my own anxious misery.

So, yes, that is the genesis of the title *Just Send the Text*. But Just Sending the Text is about so much more than hitting "send" on a rant-filled, late-at-night text to the person you've been pining over for months. It's about going with your gut. It's about rejecting the idea that you have to bend over backward to make people like you. It's about having the "What are we?" talk the minute you start wondering what you are. It's about telling them you want a relationship, even if you're worried it might turn them off. It's about responding to their "hi" text without consulting seven of your friends. It's about blocking them on social media if seeing their posts is shoving you down a toxic rabbit hole. It's about proudly letting all of your most embarrassing freak flags fly high. It's about knowing that, for the right person, the real you—red flags and all—is more than enough. Most important, Just Sending the Text is about saving your anxious thoughts and sleepless nights for something more important than some stupid boy (or girl or nonbinary person or whomever you're into).

I understand my Jack rejection story may have left some of you skeptical on the Just Send the Text method, so let me offer you one quick success story. My childhood friend and current roommate Morgan is the queen of Just Sending the Text. She's just one of those people who are naturally sure of themselves. She doesn't second-guess herself, like, ever. Especially not in her love life.

"I was purely following how I felt," she tells me of developing feelings for her now boyfriend, Rob. "We had hooked up the day before, for the first time. And we worked together, so it was one of those awkward things where if you, like, hook up once you could pretend it never happened. And so the next day I was at some party, and we were texting and doing that really annoying thing where both of you are like, 'What are you up to,' but no one was making any concrete plans, and finally I was sitting at the party and was like, 'I want to be with him, not here,' so I just texted him, out of the blue: 'We doing this or what?'

"And he literally—this is sketchy of him, total player move—had another girl in his apartment, and got that text, thought it was so forward, up-front, and ballsy, and he realized, 'I want to hang out with her, too,' and kicked the other girl out the apartment and invited me over," she continues. "I showed up with a pizza, and from then on we were inseparable, and now we have been dating for three years."

Looking back, Morgan has zero regrets. "I don't see a point in not pursuing," she tells me with a shrug. "Even if he said, 'No, I don't like you,' and turned me away, quite frankly, it's saving my time. I'm a very busy girl."

The beauty of Morgan's mind-set—and the entire Just Send the Text approach—is that she swiftly eliminated any and all anxiety by putting herself out there from the get-go. She didn't go into her relationship with Rob thinking, *OMG, I like him so much, what can I do to make* sure *he likes me back!?* No, instead, she decided that she would lay all of her cards right on the table. If he was in, great! If not, she could move forward with no regrets and no time wasted.

OK, so that covers my story and Morgan's story. But what about *you*? How is Just Sending the Text supposed to help *you*? Well, ask yourself this: *Have I ever let anxiety get the best of me when I was dating?* Actually, better yet, why not try to go through this entire checklist:

Have You Ever . . .

☐ Assumed the person you liked couldn't possibly like you back?

☐ Acted weird around the person you liked because you were so nervous?

☐ Lied about what you wanted out of a relationship to avoid looking needy?

☐ Felt like you couldn't fully be yourself on a first date?

☐ Worried your crush would immediately write you off if they saw your face sans makeup?

☐ Asked your friends, your mom, or your Uber driver what they think you and the person you're hooking up* with "are" before asking the person yourself?

☐ Purposely not watched your crush's social media story to play it cool?

☐ Hesitated to reach out to the person you like because you assumed they'd be annoyed by you?

☐ Settled because you were afraid of being single forever?

☐ Lost sleep because you were so stressed about some aspect of your love life?

☐ Acted like you liked the person less than you really did to play it cool?

---

* I'm going to be using the term "hooking up" a lot throughout this book. Just so we're all on the same page here: I don't necessarily mean "having sex with." Instead, I'm using it as an umbrella term for any form of intimacy you're regularly engaging in with someone who's not "officially" your partner. Think of it like "seeing" someone.

☐ Read too deeply into whether or not your crush watched your Insta story?

☐ Assumed that if you're hooking up with someone you like it will eventually fizzle?

☐ Gotten legitimately stressed about the prospect of dying alone?

☐ Felt like they wouldn't like you back if you were fully yourself?

☐ Been petrified of initiating the "define the relationship" talk?

☐ Checked with friends before sending pretty much every text you've ever sent them?

☐ Taken multiple screenshots of texts they sent you for your friends to analyze?

☐ Stressed about your dating app profile not being hot, funny, or cool enough?

☐ Been too nervous to make a move on someone you're attracted to?

☐ Taken longer to respond to a text from someone you like, to look cooler or less needy?

☐ Worried about exactly how to phrase an NBD text to a person you liked?

☐ Stalked a crush or an ex on social media?

☐ Gotten upset over something you found stalking them on social media?

☐ Felt like you weren't good enough for anyone because some person rejected you?

☐ Chosen to keep dating a person even after they told you they didn't want the same thing as you?

Answering yes to any of these questions means you, like me, have let your anxiety get the best of you at some point in your dating career. In other words, you've become what I'll refer to throughout this book as a Eunice. (No offense to anyone actually named Eunice—I just picked the name of the creepy girl who would watch Amanda Bynes's character sleep in *She's the Man*). A Eunice can't just *trust* that maybe—just maybe!—the person she likes likes her just the way she is. Instead, a Eunice feels like she has to play games and consult with friends and read way too deeply into meaningless social media interactions to give her some sort of clue into what her crush could possibly be thinking.

Oh, also this is probably a good time to note that a Eunice doesn't have to be a straight woman. If you're a gay dude reading this and you relate to the plight of being a Eunice, then great! Glad I could be of service! Same goes for lesbian women, straight dudes, bi folks, pansexual persons, and literally anyone else out there. However, it is important to note that this book will reflect the experiences of straight women more than any other group because, 1) I'm a straight woman and I just don't feel right speaking for anyone else's experience, and 2) straight women, specifically, have been told for eons that they have to bend over backward to make men like them; this book is here to undo the anxiety inflicted upon them by that toxic train of thought.

OK, now that we got that out of the way, let's get back to being a Eunice. I wanted to write this book for all of the Eunices out there because, while there are about a million and one BS books teaching women how to "get the guy," there's barely any literature out there on how to stop modern dating from totally and completely diminishing your self-worth. In a world where women are blasting Lizzo and sporting cute #Feminist tees, how can we still be afraid to respond to a "hi" text from a dude we like without consulting five friends and our friendly bodega clerk? I'm not a psychiatrist, but I can tell you as a reformed Eunice and also as someone who's spent her entire career writing about modern dating that Just Sending the Text is the only real antidote to being a Eunice. Seriously. Next time a situation with a guy is making you feel that heart-beating-too-fast, face-getting-red-hot, holding-back-tears feeling, try telling yourself to *Just Send the Text*. In other words, put yourself out there. Be authentic. Do the thing that feels most true to you in that moment.

Yes, doing this will up your chances at getting the guy—we'll get into this more in Step Six. But coming up with the best way to "get the guy" isn't what this book is about. This book is about taking care of yourself. Just Sending the Text is a form of self-care, right up there with Himalayan salt lamps and sheet masks. It's about adding years back onto your life by giving yourself the permission to *stop* agonizing over whether or not you're good enough for some dude whom you most definitely *are* good enough for. It's about choosing to be yourself and no one else from the get-go. If he's into you, great! Congratulations to him! If he's not, consider that bullet dodged. And would you really have wanted to be with someone who wasn't capable of liking you for *exactly* who you are?! (Spoiler: The correct answer is no.)

At the end of the day, *Just Send the Text* is about setting yourself *free* from the stressful dumpster fire that dating has become in the 2020s. Get your party pants on, because we're about to make dating fun again, baby!

Taking Control
of Your
Inner Eunice

Let me make something clear: This book is optimistic. It's positive. It's happy. It's for people who genuinely want to cut out the drama and the unhappiness that can come along with dating and, instead, *enjoy* their lives.

I know that some of you might genuinely feel that the current dating landscape has *made* you into a Eunice. You might even feel like it has set you up to fail. And, to a certain extent, *yes*, you're right. Just a few decades ago women didn't have to worry about whether or not the people they were dating were still on Tinder, their exes didn't have the option of sliding into their DMs at any given moment, and they didn't have to waste even an ounce of their energy wondering what their relationship was with the person at whose apartment they currently kept a toothbrush. There's no doubt about the fact that dating apps, social media, and the hookup culture have made dating miserable in unprecedented ways that I'll explain throughout this chapter.

But I'm also going to explain the part *you* play in that equation.

Because let's be real. *You* are the one deciding to act like a Eunice. The hookup culture didn't *make* you do anything. Neither did dating apps. And for that matter, neither did social media. It was *you* who let them tap into your own insecurities and transform you into a Eunice. And, with the help of this book, it's going to be *you* who knows how to conquer those obstacles.

So, let's go through the three main hurdles every Eunice sees when it comes to dating today and explain how you can start changing the way you react to them.

Excuse #1: "The *hookup culture* is making me act like a Eunice."
Why You're Right: The hookup culture is very much a real thing, especially for women in their twenties and early thirties. In a survey of a nationally representative sample of 254 single women conducted by YouGov[1] for this book in March 2020, within the prior year alone:

- 18 percent of single women had found themselves in relationship purgatory where the relationship never got defined, with that number jumping to 25 percent for women between 18 and 34.[2]
- 17 percent of single women had been booty-called,[3] with that number jumping to 19 percent for women between 18 and 34.[4]
- 17 percent of single women had received unwanted sexually explicit text or app messages, with that number jumping to 18 percent for women between the ages of 18 and 34.[5]
- 16 percent of single women had received a generic greeting (i.e., a "hey" text) with no follow-up, with that number jumping to 25 percent for women between the ages of 18 and 34.[6]
- 12 percent of single women had been ghosted, with that number jumping to 22 percent for women between 18 and 34.[7]

- 10 percent of single women said they'd continued seeing someone even after that person said they didn't want to be in a relationship, with that number jumping to 23 percent for women between the ages of 18 and 34.[8]
- 10 percent of single women believed a relationship was exclusive when it wasn't, with that number jumping to 15 percent for women between the ages of 18 and 34.[9]

When human beings catch feelings, it's natural for many of us to crave some sort of progression in the relationship. But the hookup culture has led us to believe that people don't want relationships anymore. It's all very counterintuitive and confusing.

If you don't want to take it from me, take it from sociologist Lisa Wade, PhD, a professor at Occidental College and author of *American Hookup: The New Culture of Sex on Campus*.

"The hookup culture tells us that nobody wants a relationship," she explains to me over the phone. But in reality, that's not true! Despite what the hookup culture tells us, most of us *do* want relationships. The 2019 Match "Singles in America" survey[10] found 63 percent of single millennials are looking for romantic love and 70 percent of single Gen Zers want to find long-term relationships.

EUNICE	YOU
"Ugh, nobody wants relationships anymore. I'm doomed."	"Actually, most people *do* want relationships. I just need to find the right person for me."

We're being told nobody wants a relationship, but we're also humans who inevitably catch feelings and wind up . . . wanting relationships. See the problem?

How It's Making You a Eunice: It's easy to see how a landscape like this would send anyone straight to Euniceville. When you have feelings for someone, the logical next step is to somehow convey those feelings to the person you like. But we're operating under a culture that tells us that the minute we *do* tell the person how we feel, they most definitely will *not* like us back.

"The hookup culture tells us that if we want a relationship, that makes us distinctly unlikable," Wade tells me. "So, the very fact of wanting one makes us somehow undesirable and those messages are pretty toxic for confidence."

With every booty call sent and every relationship left undefined, the hookup culture subtly reaffirms the idea that nobody wants relationships anymore. And yet we pull up Instagram and—boom!—our phones are suddenly flooded with what feels like a thousand and one pictures of happy couples. So, then what? Then we're left to sit with the hurtful idea that maybe people don't want to date *us*.

Cue: being a Eunice. At its core, being a Eunice really is nothing more than a failed means of self-protection. According to the You-Gov[11] survey, 39 percent of single women listed getting hurt as one of the top three dating-related fears that caused them the most anxiety. We're *terrified* of getting hurt. So terrified that it's making us physically anxious. And, as a means of quelling that anxiety, we wind up doing anything and everything we can possibly think of to protect our hearts from getting broken by a person we've been led to believe could not possibly like us back.

OK, but Stop Letting It Make You a Eunice: Like my Catholic high school sex education textbook said, "There is no condom for the heart."

That textbook was using the quote to make a case for abstinence, but I'm going to go ahead and use it a little differently here. Let's take it to mean there isn't that much we can do to stop ourselves from having our hearts broken. Like it or not, heartbreak is a part of the human experience.

At the end of the day, do any of the things we do to protect ourselves from getting hurt by the hookup culture really work? Don't we all still wind up getting hurt anyway? Is spending weeks, months, and sometimes even *years* of our lives overanalyzing everything the person we're hooking up with does or says really a better alternative than risking rejection by saying how we feel as soon as we feel it? The way I see it, there are two common ways to get hurt: 1) Say nothing and suffer silently as things seminaturally fizzle out, or 2) say how we feel and mourn after they tell us they don't feel the same.

EUNICE	YOU
sad, blasting Sam Smith alone, crying because things fizzled with person she liked	*sad, blasting Sam Smith alone, crying because things ended after you admitted feelings and crush didn't feel the same way*
"I wonder what would have happened if I told them how I felt. Did this end because I didn't say anything or because they never liked me? I guess I'll never know."	"That was awful. And I'm so sad. But at least I didn't leave anything unsaid. They knew how I felt; they just didn't feel the same. I don't have to wonder."

We've deluded ourselves into thinking option 1 is the only way to protect our hearts when, in reality, all it's really protecting is our pride. Either way, we're still getting hurt. The only difference is these things we think we're doing to "protect" ourselves are adding a dose of regret to what many of us already decided would be an inevitable heartbreak.

"So, I was seeing this guy who wasn't very up-front with me about what he wanted from the situation. We had met previously and reconnected on Bumble," Karen, a 24-year-old from Boston, told me via Instagram DM. "We went on a date and it went really well so we went on another and so forth. At first, he wasn't too open about what he wanted; but when we talked about exes, he told me he had just broken up with someone two weeks prior to us talking and they dated for over a year. I knew from then he wasn't looking for anything serious. I told myself and him multiple times I wasn't either. It got to the point where I accepted it but still loved his company and wanted to continue seeing him. We celebrated Valentine's Day together, which made me believe he wanted more than just hooking up, so of course I started to develop deeper feelings." As soon as she started to develop those deep feelings, Karen says, she "became extremely stressed" because she knew he didn't feel the same way. They were coexisting in the sort of relationship purgatory that 18 percent of the women in the YouGov[12] survey said they've experienced.

After a certain point, the stress of trying to keep her feelings on lockdown as she and the guy she had been seeing existed in this awkward in-between phase became too much for Karen to bear. "I wasn't sure how to continue seeing him without telling him," she said. "Eventually I did, and he ended it." But that's not where the story ends! A textbook twenty-first-century ex, this guy came crawling back to Karen a week later. They got back together briefly, but, once again, it didn't end up panning out.

Karen's story has all of the elements of a classic hookup culture romance. The bottled-up feelings! The false hope! The stress! The rejection! And . . . the inevitable regret. "Throughout the whole time we spent together, I was so stressed hiding my feelings and trying to just be OK with what he wanted because I loved his company," Karen explained. Now she looks back on the experience with gratitude. Karen says the whole ordeal taught her she can't change her feelings "to conform for someone else" and that trying to do so will never land her the sort of "truthful, honest relationship" she actually wants.

Even though my friend Nina, a 26-year-old living in Boulder, wound up dating the guy she was once stressing over, she still wishes things began a little differently for them. "So, before I was dating my now boyfriend, we were just hooking up for a veryyy long time," she tells me over text. "I started to really like him and completely panicked. I mean I would be so chill around him, never stressed (on the outside), but whenever I wasn't around him I was SO stressed because I would convince myself he didn't like me and this wasn't going to end how I wanted it to (with us dating). I wouldn't say I was playing games, but I was definitely trying to act like I didn't care."

Even though she was playing it *soooo* cool on the outside, Nina remembers that at her worst she would "go into full blown anxiety attack and cry over him at night for various reasons." She says the reasons could have been anything from him not calling to them not going home together even though they were at the same party. Any Eunice knows exactly what Nina was feeling. She wasn't sure where she stood with him and, as a result, her anxious mind reacted by hyper-vigilantly looking for signs that he didn't like her. (Nina's not alone in letting an ambiguous hookup situation get the best of her mental health. More on that in Step Five.)

Looking back, Nina just wishes she could have put her own pain to rest by being honest with him sooner. "I 1000 percent wish I would have told him that I wanted more way sooner than I did. It would have saved me months of tears that ended up being completely pointless, because it turns out he NEVER knew how I felt because I had been acting so chill and never said anything," she says. "So, everything I did completely backfired on ME at the end."

My friend Alex is a 25-year-old living in New York. She came over to my place one night when I first started writing this book and told me all about a guy she'd met on Hinge a few months prior. The two apparently had an *incredible* first date. "It was like the first time since I had a boyfriend six years ago that I actually met someone that I actually like," she shared over a glass of wine.

The guy even got Alex to let her guard down a little bit by showing her all the "signs" that he liked her, too. He invited her to a concert with all his friends, he brought her on a double date with his best friend and his girlfriend, and he would even joke about them eloping. (I know, I hate this guy, too).

"I really liked him, and four or five weeks in I could just feel things started to change a little bit," she told me. The *minute* Alex started getting insecure about whether or not this guy still liked her, she felt herself turning into a Eunice. "He was acting weird and then I automatically started acting weird, too, because I started to feel very self-conscious about how he was acting. The last couple times we hung out, I just was so awkward because I was picking up on what I thought was his awkward energy. Before, I wasn't even thinking when I would text him, it would be so natural. But after the awkwardness, I would go to text him and think so strategically about what I was going to say for, like, ten minutes, and then end up saying something so weird and way too try-hard."

After the perceived weirdness, things fizzled out between the two. "I honestly really regret it to this day because I wish so badly I would have been like, 'OK, what's your deal?' Even if it was a shitty truth of, like, another girl, or not liking me or something like that. At least it would be out of my head, and I would be done with it. Or I would know if he was picking up on my awkward energy and acting that way because of me. I honestly don't know.

"It just sucks," she concluded. "But now if this were to happen to me again, I would say something and just kinda risk it, even though you are putting yourself in a vulnerable situation."

To put it simply, the hookup culture had taught me, Karen, Nina, Alex, and countless other women that liking a guy means you have to do *everything* in your power to make him think you don't like him. But it doesn't have to be that way! That's the beauty of Just Sending the Text. It lets you free yourself from all of the overthinking about what you "should" be doing. You want a relationship with someone? Cool, tell them. If they want the same thing as you, great! If they don't, you just spared yourself months of useless stress and anxiety pining over someone who would have never made you happy anyway.

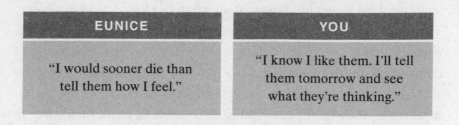

EUNICE	YOU
"I would sooner die than tell them how I feel."	"I know I like them. I'll tell them tomorrow and see what they're thinking."

The Underrated Bright Side: Part of changing the way we react to the hookup culture is changing the way we perceive it. Yes, all of the negative stuff I've mentioned is true, but the hookup culture isn't really *all* bad.

In an interview I did with her for my article "Dating + Social Media: The New Rules"[13] in the May 2018 issue of *Cosmopolitan*,* Wade actually called it "innovative." Why? Because we're taking our time to get to know people before diving headfirst into a relationship. "Young people are getting a lot of flak these days for being slow to admit they like each other or slow to commit to one another and, in some ways, I think that's really misguided. They are fearful of admitting they want commitment, but what they're doing to try to manage that nervousness is creating a whole bunch of these other tiny little baby steps that get you toward commitment because it's less scary to take a little baby step than the big step," Wade explained. "So, first you've just hooked up, then you're just 'hooking up,' then you're maybe exclusive but not in a relationship."

Yes, those baby steps help give us a much-appreciated cushion before we have to have the dreaded "What are we?" talk, but, most important, I think they give us a chance to really know someone. Imagine you went on the best first date ever. You stayed talking at the

---

* Listen, I know quoting my own work is obnoxious. But I'm going to be doing it a few times throughout the book because I want to share any info I have that might be helpful to my readers.

restaurant for hours until the manager had to kick you out at closing. Then you just aimlessly walked around talking for two more hours, which felt like five minutes because the conversation was flowing so naturally. You just cannot believe how much you have in common with this person. Not only are you insanely attracted to them, but it feels like they totally get your bizarre sense of humor and they're even obsessed with that weird YouTube show all of your friends refuse to watch with you. After the date, you go home and you tell your roommate you think you met The One. In that moment, this person can literally do no wrong in your eyes. They are as close to perfect as a human can get.

Thanks to the hookup culture, you have time to take this person off the pedestal you placed them on after that first date and get to know them in a decidedly low-stakes way. Maybe a few weeks into dating you finally go to their place only to find they unironically have a "Saturdays Are for the Boys" flag hanging above the bed. Maybe you guys decide to take a SoulCycle class together during which you learn they're the kind of person who high-fives even when the instructor isn't forcing them to. Maybe one night you suggest watching *Sleepless in Seattle,* and they say no because they "can't stand" Tom Hanks. And maybe none of these things is even a deal breaker for you! The point is the hookup culture gives us all the chance to be sure before we commit to being in relationships.

EUNICE	YOU
"OMG, that was the best first date *ever.* We need to become official immediately."	"The first date was great, but I obvi won't *really* know how I feel until we spend more time together."

Next time you start developing feelings for someone, use the hookup culture to your advantage by taking all of the time you need to make sure you've gotten to see the person for who they are. Then, if you decide you *still* want something more serious with them, apply the Just Send the Text method and *say something*. Bada bing bada boom. Easy.

Excuse #2: "*Dating apps* are making me act like a Eunice."
Why You're Right: We have so, so, so, *so* many options. All any of us has to do is spend less than ten seconds downloading an app to transform our phone into a never-ending amusement park of romantic possibilities. But that's not really the scary part, is it? No, the scary part stems from the fact that the people we're seeing also have access to these very same options.

"I think online dating has helped a lot in some ways, but I think it's also hurt a lot in a lot of ways in terms of people meeting somebody," Dr. Niloo Dardashti, a relationship expert in New York City, told me during an interview we were doing for a piece I wrote called "DUI: Dating Under the Influence,"[14] which appeared in the January 2018 issue of *Cosmopolitan*. "Ironically, I think that it's actually had a paradoxical effect in terms of people actually making connections. When you go on [a dating app], it's like a supermarket: You're just scrolling through things and people become depersonalized. So, people have probably had multiple experiences where someone ghosted them or just never got back to them and they don't know what's wrong, so the anxiety gets reinforced."

In other words, you may go on a perfectly wonderful first date and never hear from the person again. And it would have nothing to do with you! You could do every single thing right and still not have things pan out, simply because the person you met is still trying to sift through the thousands of options available to them. The way they see it, it was nothing personal. But that doesn't make it *feel* any less personal for you.

My friend Alex has a coworker whom she describes as "the *nicest* boy." Alex and this Nice Boy are both in their mid-twenties, single, and regularly use dating apps. That being said, the *way* they use apps couldn't be more different. "My personal opinion is you need to be a little selfish and look out for yourself, and still continue to be open to other options because you really don't know," Alex tells me. "You don't know a person after just a few dates. I would never want to close myself off like that." Alex tells me she wouldn't actually be exclusive with a guy she met on a dating app until they've been on *at least* fifteen dates.

Nice Boy is the kind of person who, per Dr. Dardashti's guidelines, might get hurt by dating apps. He has a *very* different view on things than Alex and many other app users—especially those in major cities like New York and San Francisco—do. "He's been kind of dating a girl on Hinge and he was feeling so bad about meeting two different girls at the same time—not even *dating* them—he had maybe been on two or three dates with each of them, and he was like, 'Alex, I can't do this.' I told him it's fine. He doesn't even know if he likes one of them yet! I was like, 'Just keep doing it and then the second you don't like one of them, you can stop it, but at least there is someone else who's in the picture.'

"So, he stops seeing one of them and continues to see the other one. They had four or five really great dates and talked a lot over the course of a month. Then on the fifth date, he asks her if she's seeing anyone else . . . and she goes yeah. He was devastated and, honestly—it's been a week or two—he probably still is."

Nice Boy's story is sad for him, but it might have also been just as stressful for the woman who had to tell him she was seeing other people. My good friend from college Nora, 28, gets stressed at just the thought of having to reject people she meets through the apps. "The biggest pressure I feel after chatting with someone on the apps is around not really liking the person that much in person and having to deal with rejecting or ghosting them after the date," she previously told me for an article for Tinder Swipe Life titled "7 Dating Pressures You Can Just Go Ahead And Ignore."[15]

Whether you're the one doing the rejecting or the one being rejected, dating apps can undoubtedly make things stressful. So much so that 27 percent of the women in the YouGov survey said they find going on a first date with someone they met on the apps to be anxiety inducing.[16]

How It's Making You a Eunice: Everything I mentioned above is stressful, but how does it turn us into Eunices? Well, for me and many other Eunices, the apps can work as a sort of Band-Aid.

Yes, a lot of the insecurity we have is born from their very existence. But the apps also have a way of soothing the sting of rejection. Compulsively swiping serves as a safeguard, ensuring we don't ever have to feel the pain that Nice Boy had to endure. I mean, how can we find the time to be hurt when we have *so* many other options to sift through? It can be our way of tricking ourselves into numbness. We inundate ourselves with options, so we don't have to be saddled with feelings.

When I liked Jack, the apps didn't exist. So, when I'd start feeling insecure that he wasn't texting me back or sad that I saw him flirting with another girl, I had no choice but to just *sit* with that feeling. The apps gave me a way out of that misery.

The summer before my senior year of college, I was interning for *Cosmopolitan* in New York and I liked a new boy—let's call him Liam. I was two years older, but a lot of those same Eunice-y feelings still haunted me. Liam would get tagged in a picture with another girl or take a bit too long to text me back and I could feel my brain starting to spiral again. But rather than letting myself go down the thought tornado, I would quickly pull up Hinge or The League or whatever app I was using at the time and distract myself with all of the many other fish in the sea. The apps made me feel like I had a small semblance of control in what I knew to be an otherwise totally out-of-control situation.

But that sense of control was just a façade. If you cut even a millimeter deeper, you could see I was still being totally and completely controlled by the fear of being rejected or hurt.

All I was really doing by compulsively swiping was creating an infinite buffer for myself to make sure I was "OK" when things inevitably didn't work out with Liam. I was, once again, setting myself up for disappointment, just in different ways than I had been before.

Listen, I'm all for using the apps to meet a ton of people and casually date multiple people at once, but only if that's what you actually want to do. That's not really what I wanted at all. What *I* wanted was a relationship. And I didn't want a relationship with just some random person I swiped right on. I wanted a relationship with Liam. But admitting I wanted that filled me with an anxious dread, and instead of dealing with that uncertainty, I used the options that came along with dating apps as a sort of makeshift Band-Aid. The apps allowed me to safely keep one foot out the door so that I'd never risk getting hurt by going all in with my feelings. But, in keeping one foot out the door, I wound up shooting myself in the foot that stayed inside. My plan worked. I never got too hurt by Liam, but in avoiding that pain, I wound up losing sight of *myself* and what *I* wanted.

EUNICE	YOU
using the apps to distract from people I actually like	*using the apps to find people I actually like*

The thing is, when I really look back on my actions during that time, I clearly see that my compulsive swiping had way more to do with *me* than it did with any issue presented by the apps. Because of my own past experiences, I just assumed nobody could possibly be interested in a relationship with me. Especially not on the apps, where there are literally thousands of options. But I couldn't have been more wrong. According to Match's 2019 "Singles in America" survey, 66 percent of singles using dating apps are open to finding a new relationship. That's compared to only 9 percent who said they're using the apps strictly for casual dating.[17] There were *plenty* of people looking for what I was looking for; I was just too stubborn to believe it.

OK, but Stop Letting It Make You a Eunice: Dating apps aren't *forcing* you to do anything or act in a certain way; they're simply providing a means to an end that didn't exist before. And, hey, if you feel like the anxiety from being on them is starting to overwhelm you . . . you can always just delete them. Conversely, if you're starting to notice that you're using them to mask any sort of potential feelings that may arise, I'd also recommend deleting them for a bit. Use the apps so long as you feel like yourself while you're on them. The minute you start to feel like they're dulling your shine or making you unnecessarily stressed, get rid of them.

Signs It's Time for an App Break

☐ You're using them to make sure you're not putting all your eggs in one basket, even though you're only currently interested in one person and have no interest in seeing anyone else.

☐ Making small talk with the strangers you matched with feels like a chore.

☐ You're constantly scheduling dates, then bailing last minute because you're too nervous.

☐ You've gone on multiple first dates that didn't lead to anything and are feeling burned out.

☐ Just the sight of them on your phone makes you stressed.

☐ You've scheduled multiple dates that never materialized and are feeling discouraged.

☐ You're using them as a distraction from some sort of heartbreak you're avoiding.

☐ You're just on there trying to get some matches for "attention."

Of course, getting rid of the apps is easier said than done for most Eunices. First, there's the FOMO factor. If we're not currently seeing someone, deleting the apps can feel like romantic suicide. It's the ultimate FOMO, right? Every second we're spending not on the apps is a second we're spending away from swiping on someone who could potentially be The One.

The other big roadblock for us Eunices when it comes to deleting the apps? In modern dating, deleting the apps has become a sort of Relationship Milestone. We typically delete the apps *for* each other once things start to get serious. And, in doing so, we've forgotten that deleting the apps can be something we just do for ourselves. Even if we're really monogamous people, like Nice Boy, who don't necessarily want to be on the apps while getting to know someone, we avoid deleting them before that pivotal moment because we don't want to be the one who went all in too soon and then got burned.

EUNICE	YOU
"I need to keep swiping even though it's making me so anxious I might vom."	"The apps are making me kind of anxious. Maybe I'll delete them for a bit until I'm ready to go back on."

Whether you're seeing someone at the moment or not, taking an app break is very much a form of self-care. It has nothing to do with who you are or aren't seeing. It's something you're doing for *you*. If you're experiencing any of the signs it's time for a break, do yourself a favor and . . . take a break. Delete all your dating apps, focus on yourself for a bit, and log back on when you feel ready and excited to be on them. Maybe it'll be tomorrow! Maybe it'll be never. Just do whatever works for you.

As for the stress of getting rejected by someone who has too many options on their phone to seriously consider you, I'll say this: Part of Just Sending the Text is knowing that for the *right* person you're about a billion times better than anyone else on the apps—or on all of planet Earth, for that matter. You're better off on your own than you are with someone who doesn't obviously see that. There will be more on how to actually believe that in every chapter of this book.

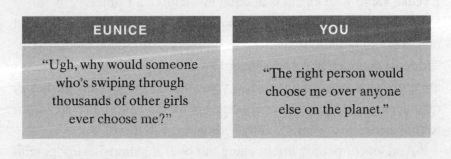

EUNICE	YOU
"Ugh, why would someone who's swiping through thousands of other girls ever choose me?"	"The right person would choose me over anyone else on the planet."

The Underrated Bright Side: The apps are actually . . . wait for it . . . a *really* great place to meet people. It serves repeating that Match's 2019 "Singles in America" survey found 66 percent of singles using dating apps are open to finding a new relationship.[18]

And did I mention the apps are literally *the* most popular way for couples—bona fide, "official" couples!—to meet right now? A 2019 study conducted by researchers at Stanford found that dating apps have officially replaced being introduced through friends as *the* most popular way heterosexual couples in the US meet.[19] In the study, they revealed almost 40 percent of couples in 2017 met through the apps, and that number likely has only gone up in the years since.

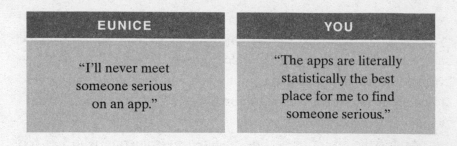

EUNICE	YOU
"I'll never meet someone serious on an app."	"The apps are literally statistically the best place for me to find someone serious."

Just take a second to let that sink in. Up until very recently, you had to sit around waiting and hoping someone would maybe introduce you to someone and that you'd maybe hit it off with them. Now you can pick up your phone and potentially meet the love of your life at any given time of the day. And if you're just looking for someone to Netflix and chill with for a night, you can find that, too.

Excuse #3: "*Social media* is making me act like a Eunice."
Why You're Right: If you want something to freak out over, social media is sitting there ready to give it to you. With social media, we're suddenly connecting with the people we're into in a way that humans were never able to up until a few years ago. It shoves our crushes in our faces every second of every day, opening a Pandora's box of potential answers to what's "really" going on with them.

And lots of people are bugging out over it. Almost every person I talked to while researching this book cited social media as being one of their main sources of stress when it comes to liking someone. Whether it's an ex sliding into our DMs or a crush who just simply refuses to watch the stories we're pretty much only posting for them to see, social media is presenting us with issues that people a couple decades ago just blatantly didn't have to deal with.

How It's Making You a Eunice: Social media can turn us into Eunices in a multitude of ways. Instead of giving a broad sweep here, I'm going to deep dive into the types of Eunice social media has the power to turn us into.

▬▬▬ THE DETECTIVE EUNICE

Signs Social Media Has Made You a Detective Eunice

- ☐ You've extensively stalked all of their exes.

- ☐ You use Snap Maps to confirm that they're actually where they said they were going.

- ☐ You're up-to-date on any people they could potentially be into that they've recently followed or been tagged in pictures with.

For 30 percent of the women in the YouGov[20] survey, social media serves as a means of finding out if the person they're into is either lying or hiding something. Take 19-year-old Haley, for example, who says social media just heightened her preexisting anxiety about her cheating ex. (For what it's worth, 13 percent of women in the YouGov survey[21] said they've dated a cheater in the past five years. But I digress. Back to Haley.) Haley explains that she knew her ex was a cheater while they were dating, but she couldn't help but hang on to the relationship because he was her first love. Instead, she just tried to use social media to keep tabs on him. "We did long distance, so it was kind of hard because I'm from New Jersey and he's from Massachusetts and sometimes I didn't know where exactly he would be because I obviously didn't live there," she explains. So, Haley decided to use Snap Maps to track him. "I became so familiar with the common places he was at, because I would always question where he was. So, I could literally recognize the buildings on Snap Maps, like I would know what they looked like and if he was there," she recalls. "Most of the time, it was at a hockey rink, but some of the time it was at a girl's house, and he would lie to me about the place that it was."

Snapchat wasn't the only tool she would use to keep tabs on

him. "And then for Instagram, I would go through the people that he was following, and click on the girls, and if they were public, I would go through all of their pictures and scroll through the pictures, and see if he liked or commented on any of them, and then question him," she says. "If he commented on any of them, I was so pissed, but if he liked them, I would question him on who it was, and stuff like that, and if they weren't public, I would look through their VSCOs and see if he was on any of them." Her ex constantly denied any claims he cheated, but eventually Haley found out that a lot of her hunches were actually true. "I continuously found out from people that it was true," she tells me. "I should have known that the comments he was leaving on other girls' photos were too intense to be just friends."

While the social media stalking ultimately led her to coming to terms with the fact that her ex was a cheater, Haley says she regrets having spent *so* much of her time and energy on it. "I am fine with the fact that it led me to these realizations about him cheating, but I regret it getting to a point where it was a bit obsessive and I had wasted my time on something I already knew to be true," she says.

Even if you're not necessarily looking for signs that they're seeing other people, a good old-fashioned stalk of your crush's profile can leave you jumping to conclusions. Like, for example, when Nina was casually stalking her then hookup buddy (now boyfriend) and came across a picture of him with another girl. "I would Facebook stalk [him] and one time remember actually bawling because someone uploaded a picture of him with a scantily clad girl and I knew the picture had been taken on a day I was with him," she recalls. I had similar experiences with pretty much every guy I liked until I changed my policy on social media (more on that soon). Whenever I'd see them tagged in a picture with another girl my heart would sink down to the ground.

▬▬▬ THE CURVEBALL EUNICE

Signs Social Media Has Made You a Curveball Eunice

☐ They comment on or even just like your picture and suddenly they're back in your head.

☐ They respond to or even just watch your story and suddenly they're back in your head.

☐ They send you a follow request out of the blue and suddenly they're back in your head.

Even when you're pretty much over the person you were seeing, social media has a way of sending you right back to square one. After things fizzled out between Alex and the guy who joked about eloping with her, he used social media to wedge his way back into her life. "We still follow each other on Instagram and stuff, and I didn't unfollow him because it's really fucked, but in the back of my mind I was like . . . maybe there's still a chance," she admits. "[I still thought this] for, like, two months, which is so fucked after dating someone for not even six weeks, that I'm literally thinking like, 'Will he ever reach out to me again?' So, I continue to follow him on social media, and I notice he wasn't liking my photos, and not viewing my stories, which is like, I know you are doing this on purpose." So, this dude keeps not watching Alex's stories for *three months*; then, right as she's starting to finally move on, he starts to creep his way back in. First, he likes one of her Instagram photos. "But I just, like, really didn't think anything of it," Alex says, adding, "At that point I was like, I think I'm, like, finally actually kind of over this."

Obvi this dude wasn't going to let her go that easily. A few days later, she posts a story of her roommate dancing, and he *responds* by sending her a DM asking where they are and what they're up to. She immediately shows the DM to her best friend. "Obviously, I tell Charlotte," she recalls. "Your best friend is automatically like, 'Fuck that, don't respond to him.'" But Alex still couldn't help but respond (don't even try to judge her; we've *all* been here). "I'm obviously going to respond; I have been fucking thinking about him potentially texting for, like, the last four months," she tells me. Alex did respond to him and . . . *nothing* came of it. Except for he wedged his way back into her mind, as planned. She was on her way to getting over him! But social media gave him the means to creep back into both her DMs and her head.

▄▄▄▄▄ THE CLOSURE-SEEKING EUNICE

Signs Social Media Has Made You a Closure-Seeking Eunice

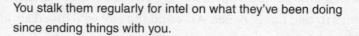

- ☐ You stalk them regularly for intel on what they've been doing since ending things with you.

- ☐ You post stories with the hope that they'll maybe respond and you guys can talk again.

- ☐ You wonder why they still watch your stories . . . or why they *don't* watch your stories.

Social media can become especially dangerous when we turn to it for closure that we weren't able to get IRL. My close friend—let's call her Penelope—is a twentysomething living in New York City. When I first started writing this book, a guy she really liked had just ended things with her. He ended things pretty abruptly and the lack of clarity left her feeling extremely anxious about the entire situation. Since she knew she'd never get any answers as to what went wrong from him directly, she decided stalking him on social media would be the only way to even slightly quell her anxiety. Her stalking app of choice? Venmo.

"I paid this one girl friend [of his] this one time, so I go all the way back to three months ago when I paid her and I click her name. I go to her friends," Penelope originally told me of her process. "I click one of her friends who I know knows him. And then I go to *his* friends. And then I get to see the person I want to stalk and see who he's paid and who's paid him. I feel like it's my homework. I think of it as a task I need to do, like it's part of my work. I'd like to think I'm normal in all other aspects of my life, but this makes me a psycho. I'm not friends with him on Facebook or Snapchat, he barely uses Instagram, so this seems like the only way to get some sort of answer as to what's going through his head." Penelope couldn't get answers from him directly, so she was desperately turning to social media to give her *some* sort of explanation of what went wrong. Unfortunately, she never wound up getting what she was looking for (more on that in a second).

■■■■■■■ **THE TAB-KEEPING EUNICE**

Signs Social Media Has Made You a Tab-Keeping Eunice

☐ You regularly check when they were last active on Instagram.

☐ You're fully up-to-date on where they are at all times via Snap Maps.

☐ You watch all their stories and are *livid* if they post one before responding to your text.

You know when your crush still hasn't responded to your text, so you go onto Instagram to see when they were last active? OK, then you know what it's like to be a Tab-Keeping Eunice.

My friend and former coworker Alexia, a 25-year-old living in New York City, is in a relationship now but admits she's used social media to keep tabs on guys she's dated in the past. "I was hooking up with this guy who always liked these meme videos from this

Instagram account, Worldstar," Alexia recalls for me over GChat. "I didn't follow Worldstar, but I started seeing '[his username] likes this' coming up in my discovery feed. I got anxious when I'd see that he liked a meme on Instagram but hadn't answered my text. Once, I think I even started following Worldstar myself, even though the content was not for me, because I'd track when he liked memes and didn't answer me. You can only imagine what that did to my anxiety."

───────────

OK, but Stop Letting It Make You a Eunice: For the most part, it's not social media that is making us insane—it's how we use it. I don't care if you're the most level-headed human being on the face of the planet, spending an hour stalking every cyber movement of a person you like is 1,000 percent going to turn you into a full-fledged Eunice. Even if you're not necessarily looking for anything incriminating, you're bound to find *one* thing that's going to drive you nuts. Maybe it's that they *told* you they were going to be at their parents' house in the suburbs all day, but you clearly saw on Snap Maps that they spent all day in their apartment in the city. Maybe it's that they've liked every single picture from an account called @bikinibuttbaes. Maybe you find out they're one of those weird people who comment "ha-ha" on public meme accounts without even tagging any of their friends in them. Maybe they commented "congrats" on their ex's best friend's engagement announcement and their ex *liked* their comment. See how out of hand this can become? With enough stalking, even a young, bright-eyed Michelle Obama would have *for sure* been able to use social media to convince herself that Barack wasn't even really that into her.

EUNICE	YOU
"I have to stalk them on social to make sure they're not being shady."	"The right person wouldn't be shady to begin with."

But thankfully, nobody is holding a gun to our heads and forcing us to stalk our crushes. We have *so* much control over how we interact with people on social media. All we need to do is exercise that control. What exercising that control looks like depends on the type of person you are. If you're the type of person who has a ton of willpower, maybe all it takes for you to quit stalking is just telling yourself you're done. But maybe you're not quite that strong.

If you *know* you're the type of person who can't follow someone you're casually dating without stalking them to the point of a panic attack, all you have to do is . . . not follow or friend them. That's what I found worked for me. After college I decided that I wouldn't be friends with guys I was casually dating on any form of social media. I stayed true to the rule until meeting my now boyfriend. I was never tempted to do any stalking while my previous almost boyfriends and I were seeing each other and, after we were done, it was nice having them just sort of fade into thin air. Even with my current boyfriend, I didn't follow him or friend him until we were exclusive. By that time, I felt like I knew him well enough that I didn't really feel the *need* to do any extensive stalking.

OK, but what if you already follow each other? If you already follow each other, and for whatever reason, having them in your social network is proving to be anxiety inducing, I'm all for blocking them, or, at the very least, hiding their posts and stories.

Signs You Need to Block or Hide Them on Social Media

☐ You have an ex who keeps trying to creep back into your life via social media.

☐ You have an ex you're constantly trying to stalk for "closure."

☐ | You can't stop stalking the person you're currently seeing.

☐ | Your heart drops every time you see they didn't watch your story.

☐ | You're really only ever posting stories hoping that they see them.

That's how Penelope was able to move on from the guy who abruptly ended things with her. Almost a year after I originally spoke to her about her cyber-stalking habits, Penelope is in a much better place. She's blocked the guy on social media, stopped checking his Venmo (well, he also became private), and moved on to a real relationship with someone who—IMO—is a much better fit for her. Penelope admits she knew she needed to block the other guy if she ever wanted to move on.

"Everyone was telling me to block him—it was advice I had given to so many other friends, so I knew it was something that I needed to do," she admits. But what ultimately pushed her to exile him from her social media world for good was her own anxiety. "I just got frustrated with that anxious feeling whenever he viewed my Instagram Story, or *didn't* view my story, or if he paid a girl on Venmo, or any of these little pieces of 'evidence' that were fueling an emotion for me," she tells me of what prompted her decision to block him. "I had read over his texts a million times, so I just kept looking on social media to find another piece of the story to figure out why he didn't like me." But that piece of the story never came along. "Social media does not give you any answers," Penelope now says matter-of-factly, adding that most of the "answers" she thought she was getting were just "illusions" created by her own anxious mind.

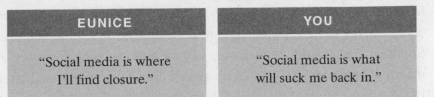

EUNICE	YOU
"Social media is where I'll find closure."	"Social media is what will suck me back in."

Blocking him didn't make Penelope's feelings magically disappear, but it did lessen her anxiety. "I'm still not completely 'healed,'" she admits. "I am definitely happy that we're not together, but I still feel the same rage and confusion, and at times anxiety, that I felt when he first ended things. But not having the constant reminder of him in my life and not having the option to look at things that remind me of him have made these tough emotions a lot less frequent." Now Penelope says when her ex crosses her mind she's able to mourn the relationship "without the added layer of stress from social media" that had previously doubled her anxiety.

I know blocking can feel dramatic or childish. But the point of Just Sending the Text is putting yourself first. You're basing your actions off how you feel, rather than how they're going to react. So, if following them is making you feel awful and you think blocking (or just unfollowing) them is going to make it better, that impulse comes above all else.

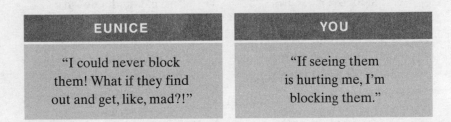

EUNICE	YOU
"I could never block them! What if they find out and get, like, mad?!"	"If seeing them is hurting me, I'm blocking them."

The Underrated Bright Side: I'm going to be honest with you, there's not much of a bright side of social media when it comes to relationships. Quite frankly, I believe dating would be infinitely better without its existence.

But, whether we like it or not, it exists. And I'm determined to find a bright side, so I'll say this: Social media has given us yet another way to make romantic connections. For example, Joe Jonas slid into Sophie Turner's DMs before ever having met her, and now they're married. Sarah Hyland and Wells Adams are also now engaged after the *Bachelor* alum slid into the *Modern Family* star's DMs. Quavo slid into Saweetie's DMs, and now they're blissfully living together. I could keep listing celebs, but I'll spare you.

The beauty of all of this is you don't have to be an A-list celeb to have access to social media. We all officially have the chance to flirt with, not only pretty much every single person we've ever encountered IRL, but also those totally unattainable people we thought we'd never cross paths with. You could set this book down right now, pick up your phone, log on to Instagram, and DM the childhood crush you never had the courage to talk to. And, by that same token, you could also DM your celeb crush. And hey! Maybe also that waiter who seemed cute at the restaurant the other night. You probably won't hear back. But there's also a chance you will. One DM is the only thing standing between a life of "what if" and a life of "well, at least I can say I shot my shot."

EUNICE	YOU
"Social media is the *worst*. It's ruining my life. Nothing is OK. I'm compulsively stalking both my crush and my ex and I'm more convinced than ever that I'll never find love."	"Social media doesn't really affect my dating life, other than the fact now I technically have a shot with Timothée Chalamet that I wouldn't have otherwise had . . . ?"

Social media has gifted us all the chance to shoot our shots. And for that we should be grateful.

———

Dating right now is by no means *easy*. All of these things I just mentioned can make it extremely difficult to keep cool and trust our own instincts. But, at the end of the day, we're the only ones who have any power over our outlooks when it comes to dating. We can choose to believe that dating is terrible and there's nothing we can do about it, *or* we can accept some responsibility and acknowledge the fact that *we* are pivotal parts of this equation. We're not going to change the popularity of dating apps, we're not going to change the hookup culture, we're not going to stop people from using Instagram, and we're not going to change whatever new nonsense gets thrown into the mix next, but we *are* capable of changing ourselves. We're capable of changing the way we react to these things and we're capable of being hyper-aware of the positive, rather than the negative, aspects of them.

Don't Be a Eunice . . .

- Just set yourself free from relationship purgatory by being up-front.
- Just view the apps as *one of* the ways you could meet someone.
- Just block them on social if you can't resist stalking them.

Rewriting Happily Ever After

In theory Just Sending the Text is simple, right? You just write some words and hit "send." Or think a thought and then say it out loud. That's it. The key to overcoming your dating anxiety is *that* simple.

But a true Eunice knows that "just sending a text" is about a billion times easier said than done. And, as we covered in the last chapter, it's not difficult because of the hookup culture, or because of dating apps, or even because of social media. It's difficult because of *you*. In this step, we'll confront the only thing truly holding a Eunice back from sending the text: her own lack of self-confidence. Somewhere deep down inside, a Eunice honestly believes she *needs* this person—even if they're totally not her type and honestly kind of a jerk—to validate her. So, she's going to try to do everything in her power to keep them, even if keeping them means sacrificing her own interests in order to seem more likable to them. (Cue: overanalyzing meaningless texts, pretending to like beer when you really prefer cosmos, pretending to be excited by baseball games, et cetera.)

The sad fact of the matter is you'll never overcome your dating anxiety if you can't accept the fact that you don't need a significant other to complete your life. How can you Just Send the Text and pay no mind to the idiot who doesn't love you exactly as you are when you think settling for that idiot is better than being alone?

The fear of being alone is a common one, especially among the single women I've surveyed. "Who, like, *actually* wants to die alone?" Haley, the 19-year-old college student who caught her ex-boyfriend cheating, asks. "Sometimes I think about it because both of my grandmas are living alone and that's just sad."

Before meeting her now boyfriend, Penelope—my friend who used to stalk her ex on social media—was convinced that she was doomed to live a sad, lonely life. "I mean, I already know I'm going to die alone," she told me one day shortly after her casual ex ended things with her. "It's just going to be a really sad life living by myself every day while all my friends have children and are married." And she's definitely not the only single woman who has been convinced that she's doomed to live that scenario.

Of course, for many of us the root of this stress is based in feeling inadequate when compared to our peers. For example, when I ask Penelope *why* she's so convinced she'll be alone forever she tells me this: "All my friends have had more serious relationships than I've had. They have the ability to be in a relationship and I don't, based on what's happened in the past." Penelope's not alone here—lots of women feel particularly insecure about their singlehood when they start comparing their love lives to those of their friends: 21 percent of the single women polled by YouGov[1] listed comparing their love lives to those of their friends as one of the most stressful parts of being single, with that number jumping to 32 percent for women between the ages of 18 and 34.

Another stressful part of being single? Feeling like your romantic life isn't measuring up to what your family thinks it should be. The YouGov[2] survey revealed 18 percent of single women found it stressful that their love life doesn't measure up to their family's expectations, with that number jumping to 25 percent for women between the ages of 18 and 34. Societal norms don't help, either—21 percent of single women noted the feeling that their love lives don't measure up to what they "should" be based on societal norms as something that stresses them out, with that number jumping to 28 percent for women between the ages of 18 and 34. From every angle, women are feeling the pressure to find a partner.

Take my friend Emily, for example. A 27-year-old living in New York, Emily says she feels generally fine about her relationship status until other people go out of their way to make her feel weird about it. "I only question it when other people make me think that way. I was in the car with my aunt once and she just let out a big sigh and said, 'We need to find you someone,'" she recalls. "I feel like I am totally capable of finding someone and know that I am not actively looking or putting myself out there, so when people make these kinds of comments, I immediately second-guess myself. It's a little discouraging because I know some people find their person at twenty-five, but some take more time, and some may not even find a person. It's like there is something wrong with choosing or wanting to be alone forever."

Nora, my 28-year-old friend from college who struggles with rejecting dudes on apps, has a similar experience with singlehood as Emily. "I wouldn't say I'm scared of being single," she says. "I'm definitely not. I think it's more the pressures of other people when you get to a certain age, like family members bugging you . . . like 'Oh, when do you think you're going to find a boyfriend?' Or 'Oh, when do you think you're going to take that next step in life?' But I personally am not scared of it. I would love to have a family and kids one day, but it's not something I've always dreamed of. I'm not thinking about my clock ticking."

These experiences with singledom are pretty par for the course in a society that paints single men as suave Leonardo DiCaprio–type bachelors and single women as spinster cat ladies. Even in an age in which men and women are supposedly equal, lots of us still have a hard time letting go of the idea that marrying a Prince (or Princess) Charming is a necessary part of the happily-ever-after equation. The cultural pressure on women to find a partner in order to make their lives complete goes back decades. "I think that there's a very long intertwined cultural and economic history that encourages women to feel this way, to be anxious and desperate about dating and achieving coupledom," notes Melissa Sanchez, a core faculty member of the Gender, Sexuality, and Women's Studies Program at University of Pennsylvania.

"Heterosexual women were taught from very early on that their self-worth depends on achieving their motherhood," she continues. "And so, to reach a certain age—I don't know what that would be for any given woman—and to still be unmarried, to still not have children, I think for a lot of women, is the worst imaginable failure."

While men who are now in their twenties and thirties likely grew up watching superhero movies and buddy comedies, women in the same age bracket were watching fairy tales and rom-coms. Their happy endings were saving the world or going on fun adventures. But ours—without fail—getting the guy. In *Sleeping Beauty*, *Cinderella*, *Snow White*, and pretty much every other princess movie we watched growing up, "happily ever after" was synonymous with getting together with a handsome prince. Even strong animated women like Mulan or Anastasia ended up with a guy at the end.

And rom-coms—the fairy tales of the teenage years—subtly shove similar narratives down our throats. In *Legally Blonde*, Elle Woods gets into Harvard . . . to get the guy. Sure, she doesn't even end up with that guy, but she gets an even better guy, so it's a happy ending. In *Trainwreck*, Amy Schumer's hot mess of a character still manages to snag herself a doctor with a good personality. In *Always Be My Maybe*, Sasha's life as a successful chef is only made complete once she finds love with her childhood crush and bestie Marcus. And the list could go on! Pick any Drew Barrymore or Julia Roberts rom-com—all of them end with the girl getting the guy. (To be clear—I love every single one of these movies.) Heck, even the "re-ality" shows we currently love, like *The Bachelor*, propel this fantasy of a happily ever after involving a woman having to win the affection of a man—yes, I know there's also *The Bachelorette*, which promotes the opposite narrative. But, um, did you know that, per a 2018 article from KQED, *The Bachelor* regularly outperforms *The Bachelorette* in terms of viewer numbers?[3] There's undoubtedly something about the "get the guy" story line, in particular, that our society just cannot get enough of.

So, after spending our formative years inhaling these stories, it's no wonder that women feel like failures when they don't get the guy (or girl or nonbinary person).

It's hard to escape the impact of these movies, shows, and books. Dr. Sanchez believes that some of us are exposed to this narrative before we're even capable of formulating our own words. "We were living in New York when I had my first son and in our same building, another female baby was born within a couple of weeks of when my son was born and everyone in the building just endlessly talked about how my son was going to grow up to propose to this female baby," she remembered. "Then another male baby was also born around the same time, and then people would joke about how the two boy babies were going to have to compete over who would get to marry the girl baby. And at some point, I made a joke and I said well maybe, the two boy babies will just get married, and everyone looked at me like I was some kind of pervert.

"And you know, these are liberal Upper West Side New Yorkers—support gay rights, all of that," she adds. "But nonetheless [they still] had this incredibly traditional, incredibly heteronormative idea about what a happy life would be for these babies when they grew up."

From the moment this little baby girl was born, she was typecast as the lead in her own romantic comedy. And it's likely that many of us were brought up to see the world in the same way. So, when we're exposed to the hookup culture during young adulthood and we find ourselves getting older and older without having even had a real "official" relationship, it becomes scarier and scarier to come to terms with the idea that "happily ever after"—at least the way that we envisioned it—might never happen.

"I'm 28 this year and have never been in a real relationship," Sophia, the Brisbane, Australia–based woman behind the podcast *My Life in Situationships*, wrote to me via Instagram. "So, when is it going to happen? Because just say I meet someone, and in today's culture of hookups, it'll take maybe six to twelve months to just be exclusive. Then we officially date for a year and toward the twelve- to eighteen-month mark, we travel and look at moving in together. Then we take another six months to settle into living before he even thinks to propose. Then it's twelve-plus months until the wedding and that's only if I meet someone now. So, I'm looking at my mid-30s and we haven't even mentioned kids yet. But if we're running on the same timeline as my current situationships do, I'm not meeting any-one decent for a while yet. So yeah, I have fears."

Sophia's fears aren't unfounded. A 2014 report by Pew Research Center found that, in 2012, the number of Americans who had never been married hit a record high, with one in five adults aged 25 and over having never tied the knot.[4] In that same report, the researchers over at Pew projected that the number of never-married people in their 40s and 50s is going to reach a new record high when never-married people who were in their late twenties and early thirties at the time of the report reach middle age. If you're more of a numbers person, let me put it to you like this: 25 percent of unmarried peo-ple who were between the ages of 25 and 34 in 2014 still won't be married by the time they reach their 40s and 50s. Stats like that are obviously scary—especially within the context of a society that's told women for decades that they essentially have no value unless they're able to snag themselves a man.

And when we start getting scared that maybe the getting-the-guy thing isn't going to happen for us, what do our friends and family do? They reassure us by telling us that there's someone out there for everyone. We just have to be patient! Love *is* out there. I mean, how many friends have said that to you? How many friends have *you* said that to? I know I've said it to dozens of my own friends.

But there's no real reason that we should be saying these things in the first place. How about, instead, reminding ourselves that it's possible to live a totally fulfilling and happy life without a romantic partner? Despite pretty much everything society has told us, women are actually really great at being single. A 2017 study by data analytics company Mintel[5] found 61 percent of single women in the UK are happy being single, compared to only 49 percent of single men.

Of course, the most ironic part of it all is that Mr. (or Ms.) Right typically comes along only after you've accepted the fact that you'll be OK without them. How many stories have you heard about women who found romantic love the minute they accepted they'd be totally fine without it? The concept isn't exactly shocking. Think about your own taste. Would you be more interested in the person who desperately *needed* you—or anybody, realy—in order to be happy or the person who *wanted* you—just you—because you uniquely enhance their already complete life? (If you picked the former, please do us both a favor and read Step Three carefully).

EUNICE	YOU
"I am terrified of being single, but it's OK because I'll meet Mr. Right one day!!!!"	"I am terrified of being single, but it's OK because I'm perfectly capable of making myself happy!"

It's the feeling that we *need* love in order to make our lives complete that catapults us into Euniceville. A 2013 study conducted by researchers at the University of Toronto[6] found the fear of being alone predicts "settling for less in romantic relationships." In other words, more than a few Eunices have decided being happy alone is such a total and complete impossibility that they'd rather commit themselves to a lifetime of getting less than what they deserve. And by "more than a few," I mean almost a quarter, as a rep for Bumble Canada told me via email. A survey they conducted in 2018 found 23 percent of women indicated they are "settling" for a less than ideal partner in their romantic relationships. (Is that really all that surprising? How many friends do you have who've settled? More important, how many times have *you* considered settling?)

The key to letting go of the anxiety that produces settling is balance: You don't need to completely "get over" the fear of being single, and you also don't need to be on a frantic hunt for anyone with a pulse willing to commit to you. Companionship is a natural human desire. It's *normal* to want to have someone special to share your life with. The desire for a relationship only becomes problematic when you perceive it as a *need*. Think of it like a cookie. Yes, you can crave a cookie from time to time. And fine! Having that cookie might even bring some joy into your life. But you don't *need* that cookie to make you happy. Not to sound like a quote from your therapist's Instagram page, but, like the cookie, a relationship should only ever be something that enhances your already complete life.

EUNICE	YOU
"I *need* to be in a relationship."	"I *want* to be in a relationship."

So, how can I convince you that you don't *need* a relationship in order to live a totally fulfilling life? How can I—one person whom you've likely never met—convince you that being single (even forever!!) could be wonderful? After months of mulling this over and writing and deleting subpar drafts, I decided the only way to make this really work is for me to shut up and let other very cool women take the reins for the rest of this chapter.

Over the next few pages I've created a collection of stories from women—some currently single, others who eventually found love after long periods of being single—who will, I hope, leave you feeling inspired. Some are my close friends, some are friendly strangers, and one is my mom. All of these women are awesome, inspirational people who have, in their own ways, managed to grow comfortable with the idea of riding solo.

Treat the next few pages as a Choose Your Own Adventure of sorts. Pick the stories that strike a chord with your own personal experiences and the anxieties that you feel around your relationship status. Bust out a highlighter, Sharpie, or colored pencil, and star/circle/underline whichever story or piece of advice inspires you the most and, next time you're feeling totally hopelessly single, reread that person's story. Kind of fun, right? Think of it like a little written-out Pinterest board of single-girl inspo.

ANN—PUTTING YOURSELF ON THE PEDESTAL

When I told one of my old bosses at Elite Daily, Faye, that I'm planning on writing a book, she did me a gigantic solid by putting me in touch with three other writers she knew who were trying to start a monthly writing group. One of the members of my writing group is a 32-year-old woman named Ann, who is truly the living embodiment of the *Just Send the Text* message. When I started collecting stories, I knew Ann had to be part of it.

"This should all be taken with a grain of salt because I'm not an expert, but I feel like I've been doing this awhile and I know what makes me feel best," Ann tells me over the phone. "I just really don't think you should have to chase anyone down. If you vibe, you vibe. And if you don't, you don't. There's nothing you could have done. You either vibe or you don't. So, you might as well just be yourself."

But Ann wasn't always this sure of herself. She tells me she met her first boyfriend–let's call him Marco–when she was in college. "He was my first boyfriend. It was very exciting. I think we were together four years," she says before adding with a laugh, "and, you know, he was pretty nice to me for three of those years." By the fourth year of their relationship, when they were fresh out of college, it was clear that their lives were moving in different directions. "I remember feeling like, 'I think I have to stick with this person through the good and the bad times, but this feels like a bad time and this feels very bad. I think I should probably get out of this.'" But Marco is the one who wound up ending things with Ann, which she says was "very, very upsetting" to her at the time. "I think I would have eventually broken up with him, but I don't know because [he was my] first boyfriend. I was so excited that somebody liked me and I did think he was really smart and successful and I was just excited that this person with such high standards had gone for me."

While Ann says she doesn't want to give Marco credit by saying his dumping her was the *best* thing that ever happened to her, she does credit the experience with allowing her to figure out what she truly wanted for herself in life. "I think Marco would have been the important one in that relationship always," she says. "Bridget, my college roommate who knew Marco, was like, 'You know, he dulled your shine. You did not sparkle around him in the way that you do around people that truly love you.' I don't think Bridget coined that term, but I do think that when you're with people that make you feel good about yourself, you're shinier."

Now, over a decade after the breakup, Ann is living her shiniest life, saying she feels no *need* for a romantic partner. Sure, she's open to having one "if it was a true partner who was going to help with the laundry and take the kids to soccer practice and really be involved," but she says she's not on a hunt for her other half. "If this [person] added to my life, incredible," she says. "That would be almost unbelievable. I like my job; I like my friends; I have this great family; I have this cool new haircut. If I met some wonderful guy who was a real partner to me, oh my God. Incredible. But I don't feel the need to find that guy."

As far as her outlook on dating goes, Ann says she's now shifting the focus to herself. "The times when I feel bad about someone not wanting to see me again, or whatever, are times when I canceled my yoga class that I wanted to go to because it fit their schedule and then I think, 'Why did I do that for this person? They're not willing to do that for me,'" she says. "Or if I wasn't really myself and I overthought, like I spent all of this time thinking, 'Should I send a text or should I not?' Oh my God, you could spend so much time thinking about how to get the other person to like you and you kind of forget about 'do you like this person?'"

Having trouble snapping yourself out of the need to make him like you? Ann recommends asking yourself the following questions: "What do *I* want? Like, do *I* like this person? Am *I* so crazy about this person or am I more concerned about this person being crazy about me?"

"I feel like it's often the other way, then you get really upset when they don't want to go out anymore, and it's not because Joe was so funny or because you really thought he was so great," she says with a laugh. "It was just the fact that Joe doesn't think you're great. Nobody wants to be dumped, but I also do think if you kind of know what you're about and you stick to that, you attract friends and boyfriends or girlfriends or whatever who actually really vibe with you and then you don't have to do all of this work to be somebody else for that person."

Ann concluded our call with a statement that I'd like to print out and hang in my living room: "I just feel like, if I start out pretending that I'm this perfect girl from a movie, then I have to keep doing that forever. And I'm not this perfect girl from a movie. I am myself and, ultimately, I would want someone to end up with *me* as I am. So, it's easier just to start out that way." Amen.

EUNICE	YOU
"Do they like me?! Oh my God, if they don't like me I'll just *die*."	"Wait. Do I even like *them*? What's this person adding to my life?"

JESS—BEFRIENDING YOURSELF

When I first started working on this book, Morgan (remember her from the intro?) told me I had to talk to her friend Jess. Jess went to high school with Morgan in our hometown and now lives in LA. Have you gone through that quarter-life "I have no idea who I am" thing? Yeah, Jess has been there, too.

"I've been single now for three years, and I've had some of the best times of my life because I was able to figure out who I was and how to love myself." Before her three-year-long period of being single, Jess was a serial monogamist, saying she "jumped into relationships really early on and therefore kind of missed this critical period of growth focused on 'what do I care about? What do I like independently?'"

As you may have guessed, Jess didn't just wake up one morning with the answers to all of these questions. She had to put in the work to get to the point she's at now, and that process couldn't really begin for her until she'd gotten through grieving her most recent ex, whom she had to split with due to circumstance. "Over time, I saw how distance and different lifestyles weighed on our relationship, that love sometimes isn't enough. It was really painful, and we grew apart, but I was able to focus entirely on my work and that helped me move on," she says. "It was a process of stages that really came from filling the holes in myself emotionally, and then working to identify what I was doing to fill those holes.

"There was still this feeling of 'Who am I?' and 'What do I care about? What do I want outside of my work?' That's where the gap was; that's what I was missing."

Once she'd identified the gap, Jess was faced with the question of how she could go about filling it for herself. "For me, it was facing my fears. It was putting myself in positions that I was uncomfortable with, which—for me—was slowing down, and being completely alone . . . that took the form of a two-week solo hiking trip where I just packed up my car and went camping for two weeks at the Tetons and the Grand Canyon." Jess knew a solo trip was her best course of action for getting some clarity.

The best part of Jess's story is that she actually did it. She didn't just hang on to the idea of this solo trip as a fantasy she'd look into on Kayak while she was procrastinating at work; she went ahead and did the damn thing. And it paid off. "I went for it," she tells me. "I had fourteen days of sixteen hours a day of talking to myself out loud on hikes, just making myself laugh, looking back at myself in the rearview mirror of my car, singing and smiling. I was completely alone in those moments, and the happiest I've ever been. That's when I realized I could be friends with myself."

Faced with herself at such an intimate level, Jess examined her inner thoughts in way that she never had to before: "I had always been so critical of myself, but hearing that voice in my head aloud for so many days alone, I realized how much gentler I could be, that I should be treating myself the way I hoped others would."

Ultimately, the process left Jess with a much deeper understanding of herself. But a few things had to happen before she was able to get to that point: "Going from serious relationship to serious relationship, I was used to taking on the needs of another human being while ignoring my own, and then when those relationships ended I just filled in the gaps with work. I saw how easy it was to distract myself from examining myself and my needs. Forcing myself to confront that head-on was one of the hardest but most rewarding things I've ever done."

Jess has since returned from the journey and has reentered her day-to-day life, which now also involves dating. But she's not done trying to fill the holes within herself. "My number one priority is myself, cultivating who I am and maintaining that feeling that I found on that trip, which is to be proud of, loving, and kind to whoever I become. For me, that means being more vulnerable and opening up to others again," she says. "I think that's my next challenge in this process, sharing my heart and letting people see the real me."

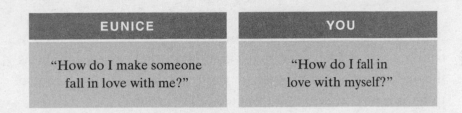

EUNICE	YOU
"How do I make someone fall in love with me?"	"How do I fall in love with myself?"

TARA—TURNING OFF AUTOPILOT

When Tara—now 40 and living in Harrisburg, Pennsylvania—agreed to get engaged to her boyfriend at 24 years old, she admits she just sort of did it because "it was like that's just what you do. It was a logical next step—we had been dating for a few years, we had been living together for about two years, when he proposed." Tara had known the guy her entire life. They started dating at 22, things started to get serious, and a couple of years later she found herself standing in front of him as he knelt with a ring in his hands.

"I remember looking at him and looking at the ring and just being like, 'OK, I guess this is it. We live together, we have a dog, we have friends together, we have a house; this is just what people do,'" she tells me on the phone. "I knew it was wrong. I definitely did not feel like, 'Oh my God, this is *The One*' . . . I felt like it wasn't the right thing, but, in my mind . . . there was just no socially acceptable reason for me to say no."

So she went through with it. "We got married; I didn't want to have a big wedding. At the time I joked that I wanted to save my money for the divorce, which should have been a red flag to everybody I knew," she says with a laugh. "So we had a destination wedding. We got married by ourselves. It was really nice." Pretty much immediately after that, things took a turn for the worse. "The problems that had always existed between us just kind of became much worse, much more amplified," she recalls. "My ex-husband had a lot of ideas about what marriage meant and that I was supposed to become a wife after that. So, it started pretty quick. One night he said, 'Oh, I want you to start taking on more wifely duties.' I was like, 'What are you talking about?!'

"He wanted me to quit my job, he wanted me to have kids, and I didn't want any of that," she continues. "He just thought—kind of a continuation of where I started—that this is what you do and this is the way it's supposed to be and it wasn't me, it wasn't who I wanted to be, it wasn't the way that I wanted to live my life."

For a year and a half, the two were in a state of nonstop conflict. "We just fought a lot for pretty much the entire marriage," she remembers with a laugh. "[It got] to the point where I was really depressed—I was sleeping as much as I possibly could; I hated him. Thankfully he worked a lot, Sunday was his only day off, so I didn't have to see him all that much. It was just really terrible."

Finally, her husband asked for a separation. "It had been really, really bad between us and he came home late one night, and he said that he thought that we should separate," she says. "At first, I was really angry, and I stomped out of the room, I took off my rings. But he followed me, and he said, 'Isn't this what you want? Don't you hate me?' And I said, 'Yeah, I do hate you.' And in that moment—when I told him I hated him—I could stop hating him finally because it changed everything. It was such a relief. I was so happy."

And to be clear, the shift really was *that* immediate. The moment Tara was free from the marriage she'd settled into she was overcome with joy. "It was so funny. A family friend of ours was an attorney in another state, so he couldn't handle our divorce, but he knew what questions to ask, so we met with him for lunch one day and so we sat with him at this Chinese restaurant and he kind of helped us work out our separation agreement and at one point my now ex-husband got up and went to the bathroom and this family friend looked at me and said, 'You're glowing,'" Tara remembers, adding with a laugh, "I was like, 'Yeah, I know!'"

The separation ultimately left Tara, who eventually found love with someone else, with a newfound appreciation for being on her own. "It was so great. I remember one of the days I was moving. My dad was there with me and he helped me set up my stereo and I put a Pink Floyd record on the turntable. I didn't have any furniture at the time, I just had this stereo in an empty room, and I sat down on this hardwood floor and I laid back and I just was so— I was so relieved and so happy and just absolutely joyful. I was laughing and crying to be listening to my music in my space. For the next couple weeks it was nothing but foreign films and canned soup because I can do whatever I want."

EUNICE	YOU
guy asks her to do literally anything	*guy asks her to do literally anything*
"Yes!!!!!!!!!!!!!!"	"Let me think about this. Do I even like you?"

CORI—MAKING THE MOST OUT OF HEARTBREAK

Cori, a 27-year-old living in San Francisco, has been one of my closest friends since high school. Cori's first relationship—which started in her mid-twenties—ended after about a year, and since then I have to say she has been the *happiest* I've ever seen her. "I truly feel like a different person than I was when I was single before my relationship, in, like, a much better way," she tells me via FaceTime. "Like, right now I'm seeing this guy and he doesn't want to officially date me. I just genuinely think about who I was before and how I would have been so in my head about it thinking that it's me, but now I know that's not what I want. It's not that I don't want a relationship neces-sarily; it's just that I know I don't want that with him."

Cori says she's in no rush to hop back into another relationship. "I just realize I like being single because I like being able to do what I want—and it's so cliché, but I actually get to focus on myself and my friends a lot more," she says. "I think when you're attached to some-one you tend to mold—and I'm not saying it happens to everyone—but lots of people end up molding into each other and losing their own personalities. Being single, you really, really understand who you are. I wish people wouldn't be so in their heads about being single. It's so much better to embrace it."

When I ask Cori how she got to this point, she tells me getting her heart broken by her ex-boyfriend did the trick. "I hope people that were like me before get their heart broken because it's truly— You learn so much about yourself," she says. "Heartbreak is the worst thing in the world, but it ends up being the best thing for you, I guess. Like, it took me a *while* to recover, but it's just, like, man, you learn so much."

For Cori, turning heartbreak into something positive wasn't something that just magically happened on its own. She says with a laugh, "You know that saying 'time heals everything'? Yeah. That's true. But you also can't sit there and just let time heal everything." (More on what Cori actually *did* in a bit).

And, no, Cori doesn't think "heartbreak" has to come from a *boyfriend*. "It doesn't have to be with someone who was your boyfriend," she says, noting that the pain you feel when ending a situationship is less like heartbreak and more like something that breaks *you*. "It breaks you because you think something is wrong with you, which is just as bad," she says. "Like, when I think about the guy I was seeing most recently before my relationship— I was never officially with him, but it was awful because I thought there was something wrong with me because he wouldn't date me. But [now I know] there's not."

With time, Cori says, it becomes increasingly obvious that what someone who didn't want to date you thinks of you is irrelevant. "Does anyone really look back on their past situationships and think, 'Damn, I wish I was still with them'? No," she says with a laugh. "You're like, 'Good thing.' I look back on those people I was so sad about and now I'm like, 'Ew. That person was so gross.'" To be clear, this is a woman who once *sobbed* to me for an entire night after having someone she was seeing abruptly end things with her. She knows what it's like to have a person whom you're seeing but not with totally diminish your self-worth. But, with time, she was able to find her own strength and see him and all of the boys who never quite made it to "boyfriend status" for what they really were—not worth her time.

EUNICE	YOU
"Shut up, Celine. My heart absolutely will *not* go on."	"My heart hurts right now, but I'll eventually come out of it with a better understanding of myself."

TIFFANI—REJECTING THE NORM

Tiffani, a 33-year-old woman living outside of Los Angeles, knows romantic relationships aren't for her. She came to the conclusion when she was 21 and briefly living with her then boyfriend. "After that, I just never really got serious with anybody. I mean, of course you meet people along the way and you try, but I never really took it to the next level," she tells me over the phone, adding with a laugh that she's not saying she's "celibate, either."

It's the emotional aspect of relationships that doesn't really do it for Tiffani. "I noticed I could never really get the idea of partnership," she says. "It's not that I'm a bad person. I just like to have my alone time, I like to do things on my own, and I don't like having to answer to anyone." As you can imagine, this proved to be a challenge when dating. "I went on dates and I talked to people. I just never could really find interest in wanting to be with someone," she says. "People would try to get me to meet people and I just never really had the desire. Even when I was trying to seriously date someone, I wouldn't feel like I was myself. It just made me feel different. . . . It's a really weird feeling because a lot of people like partnership and affection and I'm just not that way."

In a society where everyone—especially women—is expected to be "that way," Tiffani just would rather be on her own. And people have a really hard time understanding that. "I would go places with my family and my sisters would say, 'Oh, you need to get out more.' They would even try to get me to meet people and introduce me to people. I remember one conversation where my sister said, 'If somebody is twenty-four years old and they are not even thinking about, 'Oh, I want to get married,' or, 'Oh, I want a relationship,' don't you think there's something wrong with that person?' I knew she was talking about me," Tiffani remembers with a laugh. "But I was like, 'No, not really.' Even to this day, people have a tendency to say, 'Oh, you're lonely,' and I'm like, 'That's not necessarily true. I know lonely people who are in relationships—loneliness can be for anybody.'"

At 24, Tiffani decided to have a child on her own. "I knew I wanted to have a child before I was twenty-seven," she says. "But I wasn't really with anyone." So, she "made an arrangement" with a childhood friend who'd been in her life since she was 12. "I let him know that this is what I'm wanting to do. We did it the traditional way. I got pregnant and the rest is history," she says, noting that she told the friend she didn't want "too much involvement" from him with regard to the child and that he'd be free to do whatever he wanted with his life.

The decision to have a child on her own opened Tiffani up to even more unsolicited comments from friends and family. She says she regularly had people asking her how she wound up getting pregnant when they *knew* she wasn't technically with anyone. "It was the stigma of 'just another single mom,'" she says. "But it really wasn't like that. I had my career already. I had my own place. I was very independent, and I was ready for a child."

Even now, when her son is on the honor roll and she is happily raising him solo, Tiffani still gets some backlash from others. "No matter what, people are going to think the way they think," she says. "Even at the school, if he gets in the trouble just once or twice, as a second-grade boy will, it's always blamed on the lack of father in the home," which is obviously ridiculous. "He's just a child," she says. "They're going to run around the class."

So, how does she stay confident in her life choices when other people make her feel like she did something glaringly wrong? "I think it's a daily process," she says. "It's a daily practice of 'my life is my life' and 'my decisions, as long as they're positive for me and they won't negatively affect anyone else, [are my decisions].' So, I just try to keep myself uplifted. I have my own spirituality that I always try to take part in. I journal. I really just try to teach myself how to love myself and that I am normal and that I'm not the only person out there that has decided that marriage is not for me. I try to keep up with other women who are single mothers and draw from their strength."

Tiffani's story is especially inspiring because she took the rule book and tore it apart. She ignored the judgy looks and the old tropes of what happily ever after "should" look like and forged her own path. Though the road she's chosen hasn't been the easiest one, when I asked her if she feels like the life that she's created for herself is true to who she really is, she answers without missing a beat: "Yes."

EUNICE	YOU
has absolutely no desire to get married	
"But my mom got married! And all my friends are getting married! I have to get married because that's just what people *do*."	*has absolutely no desire to get married* "OK, well, I guess I just won't get married."

MOM—EMBRACING THE FOREVER ALONE

Let me paint you a picture of who my mom is real quick before we dive into her philosophy on singledom. This is a woman who regularly sends my sister and me emails with the subject line "YOUR

GORGEOUS MOTHER," with the body of the email just a giant picture of herself, no text needed. She's also been known to text pictures of herself to large groups of ten or more with super chill captions like "don't I look awesome!!!!???" Needless to say, her confidence is pretty aspirational. When I once asked her how she felt when she got rejected by exes, she responded with a laugh: "Who cares if they don't like me? I like me." The woman truly loves herself, and more important, she truly loves her life.

The last time I was home I asked my mom, who's now 69, to sit down and take me through how she came by her impermeable confidence and how she manages her love life.

My mom has been divorced twice. The first was a messy divorce with a husband whom she admits she never really loved, and the second was a cleaner but more heartbreaking divorce with my dad, whom she admits she truly loved. "Every time I got divorced—twice—the one important issue that I thought about a lot was being alone," she tells me as we sit across from each other in her living room. "So, I was weighing, 'OK, I'm going to leave, but that might mean being alone the rest of my life.' Every time I came to the conclusion by myself, weighing the bad and the good, that it was still worth it. It was better to be alone for the rest of my life. I did not get divorced thinking, 'Tomorrow I'm going to find somebody else.' I thought, 'Even if I don't find somebody for the rest of my life, it would be better than being with him.' That's my advice to all my friends who tell me they want to get divorced: 'You want to get divorced? Think about it. Decide if you're going to be happy by yourself for the rest of your life if you don't find anybody. This is a very important decision.'"

After she and my dad divorced, my mom had a few casual relationships here and there, but—for the most part—she was single. "I had two or three relationships over the last twenty years which all lasted a year or two, but then I would decide, 'OK, am I going to be happy the rest of my life with this guy or would I be happier dumping them to maybe find somebody else? The truth is I may not find anybody. I may be here all by myself.'" Every time, she came to the conclusion that being by herself would make her happier.

"Of course, there were times I wish I had somebody with me. I mean, I go everywhere by myself. I do everything by myself," she admits. "I don't need anybody. I have tons of girlfriends and male friends, too, that I'm very happy with. But it's nice to have a romance. It's nice to have a boyfriend; it's nice to go to all of these places and do all of these things with somebody you love."

Eventually, she did find that person in her now boyfriend. While the two are almost annoyingly in love, my mom still says she knows she'd be OK if he dumped her tomorrow. "I would still be happy because I have everything I love to see and do every day. He just *enhances* all of that by being in it." While my mom notes it might have been nice to have met him ten years earlier, she regrets no part of her largely single life. "I truly made a happy life for myself because I decided that's what I wanted," she tells me.

When I asked her how someone could go about creating a happy single life for themselves, beyond just "deciding" it's what they want, she suggested taking these five steps:

Reframe how you think about being single. "You have to look at it as freedom. You have the freedom to do everything you want to do in life. Your life is a blank canvas and you can write whatever you want on it."

Get financially secure. "Most important, make sure you're financially secure. Once you're financially secure, you can do whatever you want in life." An added bonus? My mom says just simply knowing you're capable of providing for yourself will give you an automatic confidence boost.

Get a hobby. More than that, she recommends finding something you "love" to do. "Find a hobby that you love to do. Some people love to paint; some people like playing music. If you have a hobby that brings you joy, then you're never alone."

Love your space. "Surround yourself with things that you love to look at and get rid of anything that's just there," she instructs, before pointing toward a bouquet of flowers picked from her garden sitting in a vase between us. "Just a few flowers in a vase. That makes me happy." She waves her arm around her living room we're currently seated in and adds, "These are all things I created for myself and I enjoy every minute of my life looking at it all."

Come up with a not-so-bad backup plan. "Sometimes I think, 'Worst-case scenario, if I have nothing and nobody, I'll just have a little shack on the beach in a warm area.' That's what sounds nice to me personally." The point of coming up with a not-so-bad backup plan is to ease that pressure and anxiety that come with life's inevitable blows. It's a reminder to yourself that, even if everything falls apart around you and you're left with nothing and no one, you won't just be OK—you'll be happy.

Going through these five steps can also help boost your confidence. "How could you not like yourself when you have a hobby you love and you're doing regularly, a room—that's all it needs to be! One room!—you've decorated with a couple of beautiful pieces of furniture, and some good music playing in the background? How could you not like that life? More important, how could you not like *yourself* for building that life?" I have to be honest—being single "forever" is really not something I ever feared. And I know that completely has to do with my mom. The chance to watch firsthand as she built an incredibly happy life for herself completely on her own was and forever will be the best gift she has ever given me. I hope, after having read this, you get to enjoy the gift, too.

Here are some additional tried-and-true tips from the ladies in this chapter for transforming yourself from a Sad Dumped Person into a Happy Single Person:

Work out every day. "I know everyone says this, but you actually have to put endorphins into your own body," says Cori. She's right. When you're sad, your brain is missing endorphins. To become *un*sad, you need to find a way to get those endorphins back. The healthiest way to do that? Exercise, even if it's just doing a few jumping jacks in your living room.

Do that thing you always wanted to do. For Ann, it was making the move to New York. And look where it got her. Now she's happier than she ever could have imagined. What's something you always wanted to do but couldn't because of your partner? Go do that thing.

Make lots of plans. "Even months out, I'd plan a trip to come visit you," Cori tells me of what she did following her breakup. "I made a solo trip to Ireland. I made plans for myself." Even if traveling is out of the question for you, try making simple plans. Even a FaceTime date with your best friend is something small you can look forward to.

Learn the lesson. Rather than looking at her marriage as a regret, Tara now looks back at it as a lesson learned. "It was a good learning experience. It really was," she says. "I've never regretted it. I needed to go through that to learn to become the version of myself that I am right now. I'm not really big on regret—I always say that every relationship was worth it, even the bad ones, because it gives you a chance to learn and I absolutely did."

Appreciate the relationships you *do* have. "People often overlook their friends as equally as valid if not more important relationships in their life," says Jess. And I could not agree more. Partners will come and go, but your friends and family are forever. The term "single" implies you're alone, when that's not the case at all for most single friends. Take this time to cultivate the network you *do* have. Talk to your best friend on the phone for hours; FaceTime your parents; check in with that friend you haven't spoken to in way too long. Remind yourself that you're not alone.

Go on a social media cleanse. After getting broken up with by her boyfriend, Cori decided to temporarily delete Instagram so she could avoid having him pop back into her life. "I gave my password to my friend to change and can't go back on because of that," she says. "Now [over a year later] I don't even want to go back on and it has nothing to do with him. It just makes me feel free and better about my life."

Redecorate. Take my mom's advice here and really turn your space into something you love, whether that means just picking up a few flowers from Trader Joe's or redoing your entire bedroom. Even just the activity of actively searching for pieces you adore or crafting different decorations you love will be a positive distraction from what you're going through.

Find someone you can talk to. For Cori, that meant going to therapy. "I think the breakup and the relationship made me realize what I needed to work on really badly. I should have gone to therapy before, but it really does help a lot." If therapy's not for you, don't sweat it. Cori says talking to a friend can be just as effective. "Even just talking about it to your close friends—those who aren't going to be annoyed with you for talking about it—can make a huge difference."

EUNICE	YOU
"OMG, I cannot die a lonely spinster cat lady."	"Wow, can you imagine the incredible life I could make for myself without some dude holding me back?!"

I know I'm not going to be able to undo everything society has taught you about being single. As I outlined earlier in this chapter with the help of Dr. Sanchez, there are plenty of forces much larger than this little book working to make you believe you *need* to get a guy to be happy. Obviously, one book isn't going to undo a narrative you've been force-fed your entire life.

But I hope that—at the very least—this chapter was able to give you an alternative narrative to happily ever after. Maybe next time your nosy aunt is grilling you about how you can possibly *still* be single, you can reread this chapter and remember you're perfectly capable of being your own knight in shining armor.

Don't Be a Eunice . . .

- Just let yourself crave a relationship, then let that craving pass.
- Just remember you're better off alone than settling for a dud.
- Just do whatever the heck you want, because you've got *no one* holding you back.

Stop Wasting Your Time

There are some people you just shouldn't Just Send the Text to, unless that text is "bye." As someone who's spent her career researching and writing about all things dating, I have a lot of people who come to me to ask what's wrong with them in terms of their own dating lives. The funny thing is that, for most of these people, the only thing holding them back is their own horrific taste. It's not their personality or their looks or their education level or whatever random thing they've decided is the thing makes them unlovable. It's that they're choosing to chase people who aren't worthy of their time and, in the process, diminishing their own self-worth. So many of us willingly sabotage our own lives by trying to convince horrible people to love us back. It's a colossal waste of our time, which is ironic because lots of us live in fear of wasting our time. The You-Gov[1] survey found that 37 percent of single women said the idea of "wasting time" when it comes to dating makes them anxious. In order to stop wasting time, it is IMPERATIVE—Yes, imperative! In caps!—that you remove certain people from your love life.

I've come up with a little metaphor to really highlight the importance of doing this, but fair warning, it's disgusting. (I read it out loud to my mom, and she begged me not to include it in the book. Then I read it to my dad, who's generally cooler with my more out-there ideas, and even he agreed it was disgusting. But I love it and my editor is cool with it, so here we are. Sorry, Mom and Dad.) The fact of the matter is, if you choose to waste your time chasing the wrong people, your love life—and subsequently your *entire* life—can become disgusting. So, I needed an aptly repulsive metaphor to capture just how toxic certain people can be to your life. Without further ado, I present the toilet metaphor:*

Think of your brain as a toilet. Not one of those fancy Japanese toilets with a built-in bidet and butt heater. No, think of it more as a 1960s toilet inside the bathroom of a dinky apartment in a fourth-floor walk-up. It's fine; it gets the job done. It even has a little bit of personality that newer, more modern toilets don't seem to have. But, at the end of the day, it's delicate. Sure, you can occasionally manage to flush one or two tampons down it successfully. But by the third time you try to flush a tampon down the toilet, it's officially clogged. Your bathroom is a mess, and you're desperately trying to call your super to rush up and help you unclog the toilet. It's a stinky nightmare.

Now time to break the metaphor down for any of you non–English majors who may be a little lost:

> **The toilet is your brain.** Like a toilet, your brain is in charge of processing whatever you present it with. How your love life affects your brain is up to you. You can keep things flowing smoothly by only feeding it small, neatly folded pieces of toilet paper—a metaphor for nice people who actually respect you—*or* you can give yourself a Peak Eunice Level Nervous Breakdown by feeding it an endless stream of human tampons that you *know* it can't handle.

---

* Have to give a shout-out to my college roomie Meg for not being disgusted and, instead, really helping me fine-tune this.

The tampons are toxic people in your life. If the toilet is your brain, then tampons are toxic people in your life. In other words, you brain simply cannot process them. Don't be fooled by the one it managed to successfully flush down once. Or by your friend who *swears* her toilet flushes them down just fine. Your toilet will get clogged by tampons. And as soon as that happens the entire bathroom—your life in this scenario—is filled with nasty overflow.

The nasty overflow are your anxious thoughts. In the beginning, your anxious thoughts and insecurities are overshadowed by the thrill of getting that one text back (aka the one tampon you managed to flush). You're so excited that you forget that they're all hidden deep down in there. But you keep talking to these jerks and, eventually, your brain can't take it anymore. It explodes. All of the memories of all of the jerks who've hurt you before come flying right back out alongside all of your own insecurities.

The bathroom is your entire life. Obviously, the anxiety doesn't *just* affect your brain. It affects your entire life. You stop being able to focus at work. You stop being able to be present with your friends. You stop being able to sleep. It's not good.

The super is your therapist. Or your friends. Or your mom. Whoever it is—your super in this metaphor is the person you turn to to help unclog your brain when it gets clogged by yet another jerk.

If you're wondering why I'm even bothering talking about relationships in a book about being *single*, it's because I know that being "single" doesn't necessarily mean you don't have any sort of romantic interest in your life. Instead, being "single" in modern dating usually means one of four things: 1) You're not seeing or interested in anyone; 2) you're dating around but are not really interested in anyone; 3) you're unofficially dating someone that may turn into something official; or 4) you're colossally wasting your time pining over someone who—for one reason or another—is about to make your life totally and completely miserable. This chapter focuses on that last group, aka the tampons clogging up our toilet brains.

Just one note before we get into it: I didn't include more serious red flags, like abuse, on this list because I'm not equipped to give real advice to people going through that and also think it would be massively insensitive of me to chalk up any sort of abusive relationship to a "waste of time." That being said, casual relationships can be just as abusive as "official" relationships. If you are in any sort of relationship that you feel is abusive, there are people who *can* help you. Call the National Domestic Violence Hotline at 1-800-799-7233.

OK, now time to dive in. Feel free to skim through until you find the type of person who's currently making your life a waking nightmare. Maybe you'll even see a few familiar exes who wasted your time in the past. Heck, maybe you'll even know someone who fits a few of these bills.

Whatever the case, read along, take notes, and get ready to unclog your toilet of a brain for good.

THE "THEY'RE PERFECT, BUT" PERSON

Definition: In life there's always going to be that person who's absolutely perfect for you with the exception of one huge element that's totally out of your control. They're perfect for you, "but" their job requires them to work one-hundred-hour weeks and they have no time to ever see you. They're perfect, "but" they're in the middle of a really messy divorce. They're perfect, "but" they live across the country and have no intention of moving. The "But" Person can often be the most difficult person to cut out of your life because, well, it can feel like there's no real reason to cut them out of your life. They're perfect, right?

IRL Example: I met my "He's Perfect, But" guy—let's call him Paul—at a divey New York bar when I was 22. All my friends are probably rolling their eyes as they read this because Paul effectively wasted almost a year of my life. There will be way more on him and other "but" people later on, but here's the TL;DR: Paul and I really hit it off immediately and subsequently wound up nonstop talking to each other every day for almost a year. The catch? He didn't live in New York, where I definitely did live. I tried so hard to make it work. We planned visits, we'd text each other constantly, et cetera. But the fact of the matter was it just was never going to work. He didn't live in New York. I did. And neither of us had any intention of changing that.

Why They're a Waste of Your Time: Whatever the reason behind your circumstantial "but," the bottom line is that something greater than the two of you is working against your relationship. Yes, it would be great if love really conquered all. But sometimes it doesn't. Staying with this person is only going to leave you exhausted, cynical, and hopeless. Most important, keeping them around is going to close your eyes to all of the great potential partners who *don't* come along with loads of circumstantial baggage.

Escape Plan: I know from personal experience how horrible and seemingly impossible it can be to break things off with someone you get along with so well. Despite what all of your friends and family are likely telling you, you've kept them screwed tightly onto a pedestal in your mind's eye. So how do you even begin the process of jimmying them off? I suggest keeping a notebook for two weeks where, every night before you go to bed, you mark whether you were happy that day or not. Be brutally honest. If you find that bending over backward to try to make this relationship work is making you happy, great! Congratulations: You proved me wrong. But I have a feeling it's not. And the hard truth is that this "but" situationship is never going to make you truly happy.

Use your findings from that two-week period as your ammunition to end things. As far as *how* to end things goes, you probably owe this person an explanation. Luckily, you have a logical one: This just isn't going to work. And if you're super heartbroken after you do end things, that's OK! Let yourself feel heartbroken. But eventually your heart will start to heal and you'll find that your life is infinitely less dramatic and stressful without that "but" in it. Hey, you may even meet someone you can date without having to move mountains.

Signs You're Falling for a "They're Perfect, But" Person

☐ Your friends and family are worried.

☐ You get super defensive anytime you describe your relationship.

☐ You genuinely think they can do no wrong.

☐ You're quick to make up excuses for any of their less-than-perfect behavior.

☐ There are circumstantial things getting in the way of you two ever becoming official.

☐ You believe you guys would be official if those circumstantial things didn't exist.

☐ You know deep down inside this can't go anywhere.

☐ You're starting to feel super cynical about life in general.

☐ You are putting *a lot* of effort into making this work.

☐ Your new life motto is "love conquers all."

EUNICE	YOU
"This 'relationship' is giving me stress acne and making all my friends want to put noise-canceling headphones on every time I speak, but it's OK because love conquers all!!!!!!"	"Hm, love may not be able to conquer the fact that we live fifty thousand miles apart and neither of us has any intention at all of moving."

THE TOO-MUCH-TOO-SOON PERSON

Definition: The Too-Much-Too-Soon Person goes all in right from the get-go. At their most extreme, they're showering you with grand gestures and making you feel like you're finally the star of your very own rom-com. At their most tame, they're a textbook codependent[*] relationship person who just wants to lock you down ASAP, after having ended their last relationship twenty minutes ago. Either way, they're super intense and, while you do feel special, something deep down inside warns you something is off with this person.

IRL Example: "He told me he loved me on our second date," Linsey, a 29-year-old from Omaha, told me via Instagram DM of her too-much-too-soon guy. "[It was] after quite a few drinks, but still it was crazy, and I was like what just happened? I still ended up dating him for five months. At about 4.5, it fizzled fast. He started acting aloof and then one day quit answering my calls and texts altogether."

---

[*] Twelve percent of women in our YouGov survey said they had codependent partners in the past five years.

Why They're a Waste of Your Time: I'll spare you the heartache and tell you what's off right now: They are too impulsive. Odds are, they'll be just as quick to drop you as they were to dive into the relationship. One more thing? They don't even really *know* you. Grand gestures are super flattering coming from someone who wants to knock the socks off of the real you. But this person seems to be way too excited just to be on a date with anyone with a pulse.

Escape Plan: You have two options here, depending on how you feel about the person.

Option One: End things immediately. Do this if you're getting any sort of cringeworthy gut feeling. As far as *how* to end it in this case, do what feels right for the situation—ghost them, send a nice text saying you're not feeling it, et cetera. The good thing about too-much-too-soon people is they show their true colors early on, making it easy for you to end things without having to owe them any sort of explanation.

Option Two: If aside from the intensity you're feeling into them, you can just ask to slow things down a bit for you so you really get to know each other before going all in. If they seem defensive when you ask this, run.

Signs You're Falling for a Too-Much-Too-Soon Person

☐ You get some variation of a "miss you" text five minutes after your first date.

☐ Your friends are thoroughly creeped out.

☐ You've barely told them anything about yourself and yet they swear you're The One.

- ☐ You get a cringeworthy feeling deep down inside when you think about them.

- ☐ You are kind of scared to end things with them because they're *so* intense.

- ☐ You know they've been in back-to-back serious relationships and are itching to jump into their next one with you.

- ☐ You were totally caught off guard when they dropped their first L-Bomb.

- ☐ You've barely stored their name into your contacts and they're already asking to be official.

- ☐ You notice they're just as impulsive in other areas of their life.

EUNICE	YOU
"OMG, wow. We are so in *love*. This is *it*. . . . I mean, I have a slightly nauseous pit in my stomach every time they talk about our future and my friends are super weirded out, but it doesn't matter! We're in love! It's us against the world, baby!"	"This person clearly has no grip on reality, so I'm going to take everything they say with about five thousand grains of salt."

THE DEAD END

Definition: This person is a Dead End because there is no future with them. You might be thinking, *But Candice, isn't there no future with any of these types?!* Well, in a sense, yes—but with this person, it is abundantly clear that things are not headed toward a relationship because they've blatantly told you. Whether they "don't believe in labels" or they're just "too busy for a relationship right now," the fact of the matter is seeing them is just like being trapped driving circles within an emotional cul-de-sac. And, for what it's worth, it's a cul-de-sac many other women have driven around: 18 percent of the women in our YouGov[2] survey said they had—at some point within the past five years—dated a someone who refused to fully commit.[*]

IRL Example: "I was basically 'dating' this guy for nearly two years," Brooke, a 25-year-old from Fort Worth, tells me via Instagram DM. "I was his girlfriend without the title because he could never fully commit and yet wanted all the perks of having a girlfriend. Met his family, told me he loved me, saw a future with me, etc. But every time I tried to take it to the next level with a title, he told me he 'wasn't ready.' Somehow, I was always trying to convince him that I was worth it. He was both my best friend, my faux boyfriend, and my biggest obstacle. Anyway, after nearly two years I drew a line in the sand and told him I couldn't be in this gray area anymore and he needed to figure his shit out. Our communication grew dim and within a couple months he found himself a girlfriend. They started dating and he immediately labeled them publicly and everything. It sucked."

Why They're a Waste of Your Time: Letting go of a Dead End can be just as difficult as letting go of the "But" Person. You guys may have out-of-this-world chemistry that makes you desperately want to ignore the bright red flags waving right in your face. But facts are facts. The bottom line is that being with them is committing to a life

---

[*] That number was especially high for women ages 18 to 34, with 26 percent of them saying they've experienced this at some point in the past five years.

that is in some way less fulfilled than what you want. In other words, it is a colossal waste of your time.

Escape Plan: As hard as it may be to cut ties with this person, you have to do it as soon as humanly possible. The more time you spend emotionally invested in them, the more of your precious time you're wasting. And the more of your precious time you're wasting, the more anxious you're getting. For that reason, you need to be out.

Heads up! This person is a master at having their cake and eating it, too. They're used to getting their way with no objections. As a result, they might try to convince you to stay by asking you why you can't just be cool with keeping things the way they are. Do. Not. Buy. In. Because you're obviously not at all cool with things the way they are. Because like, c'mon, you're currently reading a book to help you with your dating anxiety, which I'm willing to guess was largely caused by your relationship with this person.

Signs You've Fallen for a Dead End

☐ You try to "live in the moment" because thinking about the future with them makes you want to vomit.

☐ You question if they don't want a relationship in general or they don't want a relationship with *you*.

☐ You conveniently leave out certain things they say when talking about them to your friends.

☐ You're constantly doing mental gymnastics to justify the huge red-flag things they've said to you.

☐ You are on the lookout for any "signs" that maybe they actually do want the same thing as you.

☐ You avoid bringing up certain topics because you're afraid of their response.

☐ . . . Either that ⌃⌃ or you're constantly talking in circles about what you "are."

☐ You're hanging on to a hope that they'll change their mind.*

☐ You have told them you're cool with things as they are, even though you aren't.

☐ Your friends are over hearing you complain about this predicament.

EUNICE	YOU
"Yes, this guy has blatantly told me he doesn't want a relationship with me. But why don't I just spend the next five to ten years of my life trying to change his mind?"	"I liked him, but it doesn't look like we're searching for the same thing. Sad . . . But oh well. Better off being on my own than wasting my precious time trying to change his mind."

THE PLAYER

Definition: Do I really need to define this one? You know what a Player is—the shady person who just can't seem to go ahead and pick

---

* This is a common predicament—17 percent of all women YouGov surveyed said they've settled on a compromise for the type of relationship they're having in hopes their partner's feelings would change over time. That percentage was especially high for women in the 18 to 34 age group—20 percent—and even higher for women in the 35 to 54 age group: 23 percent.

you over the other people they currently have on their roster. The one who, even after months and months of casually dating, will grace you with a "u up" text at 4:00 a.m. on a Tuesday. If that. And let me give you a sneak preview of whom the player most likely turns into on the off chance they're able to go from hookup buddy to "official" partner: the Cheater.

IRL Example: I went through a phase when, for some reason, I was only attracting Players. There was one guy who would regularly invite me to parties at his place, and every time I'd show up, I'd notice there were about twelve other girls he was talking to *also* on the guest list. There was another guy who spent an entire night out with me at a club in Barcelona; at one point we even left the club together to go for a romantic sunrise walk outside. Then, just before we kissed, he goes, "I hope you don't mind I have a girlfriend." Oh! And finally, there was one guy who asked me out while we shared a cab to the West Village together from Penn Station. We texted— and by "texted" I mean I received booty calls from him for months without any sort of date materializing—until, finally, we ran into each other again at a bar in Montauk. We were flirting and I was kind of feeling it until a girl pulled me aside and told me that, not only had he slept with at least two women a night for the past week, he was also "known" for sleeping with women and never talking to them again. She knew because it had happened to two of her friends.

Why They're a Waste of Your Time: I have a theory that I like to call the Hailey Bieber Effect. In other words, lots of Eunices have this fantasy in their minds that they're going to take this notoriously awful Player (think: Justin circa Selena) and turn them into Husband Material. It worked for Hailey, but—you guys—she is the exception to the rule. Don't waste your time hoping to convince someone to choose you over the rest of their options. You are an obvious choice. You deserve to be with someone who knows that without having to mull it over.

————————

Escape Plan: If you don't have any real feelings and are just keeping them around for some casual fun, then sure. Have your fun! Just please be safe and don't be surprised if one day you don't hear from them again.

But if you're even slightly starting to develop feelings for this person, it's time to run before you get hit by the massive freight train of drama and anxiety headed in your direction. I personally wouldn't try to give them too much of an explanation because Players tend to be smooth talkers who can suck you back in with ease. Just try your best to let it fizzle out naturally. If that makes them even more aggressive about pursuing you, tell them point-blank that this isn't working for you. Then leave it at that.

Signs You're Falling for a Player

☐ You rarely hear from them before 10:00 p.m.

☐ You have a sneaking suspicion 80 percent of the texts they send you are also being copied and pasted to other options they have on the table.

☐ You have found some suspicious things at their apartment (i.e., a bra that wasn't yours, mysterious condoms in the trash, et cetera).

☐ You have a strong physical attraction to them, whether it be because they're really hot or they have mad game (or both).

☐ You might have a friend or two who have also hooked up with them at some point.

☐ You've watched them flirt with someone else at a party they invited you to.

☐ You've heard some not-so-great rumors about them.

☐ You got *warnings* about them from multiple people.

☐ You've noticed their actions never really match up with their words.

☐ You choose to ignore all of the above because you feel like you'll maybe be able to change them.

EUNICE	YOU
holding back loud, hysterical sobs "No, I'm totally cool with this! Seriously. Don't hate the player; hate the game! Ever heard of that little ditty? That's their–er–*our* motto!"	"Ew, gross. Why would I waste my time stressing over some indecisive idiot who can't even pick me over the rest of the one hundred people they're currently talking to?"

THE EXCUSE MACHINE

Definition: If there was an award for the Least Accountable Person on the Planet, this person would be a shoo-in. The Excuse Machine takes zero responsibility for any of their actions. For every mistake they make or hurt that they cause, they have an excuse for why it totally wasn't their fault. They have an excuse to get out of every event or activity or responsibility. You're never going to get a straight-up explanation from them, and more important, you are most definitely not going to ever get an apology. Oh, and lots of women have been there: According to our YouGov[3] survey, 21 percent of women said they've dated someone who never took responsibility.

IRL Example: "The first few months into our relationship, I booked a hotel for a night away before Christmas, which was my treat. I just get a text back saying 'that sounds lovely but I've got plans that night,'" a 30-year-old woman living in London—let's call her Jenna—tells me of her Excuse Machine via Instagram DM. "It turns out he didn't have any plans." The same thing went for multiple situations throughout their relationship. "I always tried to get us to eat out for a change and he would always say 'that sounds lovely . . . but I can cook for us at home.'" He conveniently always had a reason why he couldn't do the things she wanted him to do—a textbook Excuse Machine.

Why They're a Waste of Your Time: In addition to just being incredibly annoying, the biggest issue with the Excuse Machine is the lack of accountability. How can you actually have any sort of functional relationship with someone who doesn't think they're capable of making any sort of mistakes? Confronting them about anything is bound to feel like repeatedly banging your head against a brick wall.

Escape Plan: Just wait until the next time they try to feed you another one of their BS excuses. If they're a true Excuse Machine, you probably won't even have to wait that long. Once they inevitably make the excuse, call them on it and be done.

Signs You're Falling for an Excuse Machine

☐ You get a five-minute-long explanation for why they're late, instead of a simple "I'm sorry."

☐ You repeat their excuses to your friends.

☐ You feel like you're constantly being blown off (because you are).

☐ You have a sinking feeling that they're going to bail every time you make plans.

☐ You have caught them in multiple lies.

☐ You don't even bother calling them out on anything because you know they'd never admit to it.

☐ You have listened to them spend hours complaining about why everyone else makes life so hard for them.

☐ You have watched them make a million plans, even outside your relationship, that they never followed through on for one reason or another.

☐ You get embarrassed repeating their excuses to your friends because you know they're such BS.

☐ You don't trust them.

EUNICE	YOU
"He's too tired to be my date to my sister's rehearsal dinner tonight that I invited him to five months ago? Cool, cool, cool, cool. Totally fine. Sounds legit! Sleep is important!"	"Is this guy for real? How dumb does he think I am?! No way I'm falling for his BS. See ya later, bye."

THE BAD REF

Definition: The Bad Ref refuses to make the *right* call and put you in first place when it comes to their priorities. Heck, not even first! You're lucky if this person even puts you in their top five. You know you're seeing a Bad Ref if you feel like you'd drop plans to see them and they probably wouldn't even pause a Netflix show they were barely paying attention to in order to answer your call. If this description is hitting close to home, that's because you're not alone — You-Gov[4] found that 19 percent of the women surveyed said they've dated someone who didn't prioritize their relationship, with that number jumping to 24 percent for women between the ages of 18 and 34.

IRL Example: I have a friend who once had a guy she was seeing straight-up tell her that right now his focus was on work, his family, his friends, *then* her.

Why They're a Waste of Your Time: No, I don't think you should be the center of someone's universe — and definitely not at the beginning of a relationship (see Too-Much-Too-Soon Person). But you should at least feel like you're one of their top priorities, especially if they're one of yours.

The Bad Ref can often be the most problematic person for a Eunice or someone with Eunice-like tendencies. Why? Because they're playing into all of your most deeply rooted insecurities. By placing you at the bottom of their priority list, they're reinforcing your (false!!!!) belief that you don't deserve to be at the top.

Your Escape Plan: First of all, you need to end this toxic situationship ASAP. Don't just sit around waiting to hopefully make your way to the coveted number one spot on their priority list. If you're consistently feeling like you're the only one making any effort and prioritizing the other person, get out immediately.

In this case, I would assert yourself a little bit by telling the Bad Ref straight-up that you're ending things because you know you deserve better. Say the words out loud. Talk the talk so you can walk the walk. I see this end as a two birds–one stone type situation—you're gaining respect from them *and* from yourself.

Signs You're Falling for a Bad Ref

☐ You have dropped plans for them, but they have never done the same for you.

☐ You are afraid to ask them to do things because you know they'll just say no.

☐ Your friends and family have heard all about them, but their loved ones barely know your name.

☐ You get maybe one text back for every ten you send.

☐ You always feel like you're trying to win over their attention.

- [ ] You only get invited to hang with them on off nights when they have nothing better to do.

- [ ] You only ever Netflix and chill with them.

- [ ] You drunk text them every time you go out, then cry when they ignore you.

- [ ] You're in an Uber to their place before you can even drum up a response to the "u up" text they likely sent you just because they're bored.

EUNICE	YOU
"Yes, I've sobbed multiple times because he made me feel smaller than an ant. But that's what I'm into! That's my type!"	"I have better things to do than chase this dude who very obviously could not care less about me."

THE FISHER

Definition: I'm calling this person the Fisher because—whether it's intentional or not—they know how to keep you on the proverbial hook. Even months after the two of you have ended things, the Fisher finds a way to pop back into your life and reel you back in—whether it be with a DM on Instagram or a "miss you" text. I'm an optimist, so I like to give the Fisher the benefit of the doubt, and so I hope that they only do what they do because—at their core—they're people pleasers. They're incapable of just letting you hate them, so they periodically check in to make sure you don't. But that doesn't mean that you have to accept their actions and settle.

IRL Example: I have a friend (whom I'm going to leave nameless) who might as well be a nice hundred-dollar hunk of branzino considering how many Fishers she attracts. None of her exes really ever go away—whether it be her cheating high school ex-boyfriend who seems to pop back into her life every time she's totally over him, or her most recent long-term hookup buddy who still sends her long, heartfelt texts over a year after telling her he wasn't ready for a relationship.

Why They're a Waste of Your Time: Here's the thing. If this person really cared about you, they'd let you hate them because they'd know that is the only way you can move on. After all, the only person they really care about is themself. They're not checking in because they care about your well-being or even because they miss you; they're checking in to ease their own conscience. They feel bad about however things last ended between you guys and they selfishly want to check in to make sure you're not mad at them.

And that's the optimistic take on it. At worst, a Fisher is just a total douchebag who's purposely keeping you around as an option. Either way, they're selfish and a waste of your mental energy. I mean, how can anyone hop aboard that roller coaster and *not* turn into a Eunice?

Escape Plan: Of the types on this list, the Fisher is inarguably the most difficult person to shake. I like to think of the Fisher as the human version of the mouse that gets in your house and stays there no matter how many times you try to exterminate it. So, yes, it might be hard to completely get rid of them. They may be so ingrained in your life at this point and you might have to take extreme measures to really fully cut them off. Do what you have to do—tell them point-blank that you don't want to talk to them anymore (Warning: They'll majorly guilt you for this), unfollow them, block them, whatever it takes. But whatever you do, *don't* feel guilty. They've disrespected your wishes for ages in an attempt to do what feels right for them. Now it's your turn to do what feels right for *you*.

Signs You've Fallen for a Fisher

☐ You've had a million serious "talks" that never went anywhere.

☐ Your friends and family are over hearing about them.

☐ You guys have "ended things" with each other multiple times.

☐ . . . And yet you still have never really ended things.

☐ You get a text from them the *minute* you think you've moved on.

☐ You can't decide if they secretly love you or if they don't care about you at all.

☐ You've at some point changed their name in your phone to some variation of "don't answer."

☐ You've blocked and unblocked them multiple times.

☐ You've had entire days turned upside down because they responded to your story.

☐ You've had entire days turned upside down because they *didn't* respond to your story.

EUNICE	YOU
"Of course I'm gonna respond to their 'miss you' text! It would be rude not to!!!"	*hits "block" the minute they pop back in, proceeds to go about day normally*
proceeds to spend rest of day convincing herself things will work this time around	

THE HUMAN VOID

Definition: This type is called the Human Void because talking to them about anything serious feels like screaming into the abyss. Sure, the banter may be great. But when it comes to having any sort of real conversation, they totally shut down. Way too many women put up with this—YouGov[5] found that 28 percent of women have dated someone with poor communication skills within the past five years, with that number jumping to 38 percent for women between 18 and 34—and this needs to end now.

IRL Example: "This was definitely my last relationship," Mariah, a 22-year-old from Vancouver, tells me via Instagram DM. "Any time there was a disagreement, he would put on headphones and 'zone out' to videogames and completely ignore me even if I pushed to fix it. He also would get up and leave (we lived together) when it got bad, even knowing I have dealt with abandonment before." One more thing? Mariah adds he "claimed to 'not have emotions' when we tried to talk about anything deep."

Why They're a Waste of Your Time: You guys, c'mon. I understand Euniceville can do weird things to our judgment, but this person is just objectively bad news. What's the best-case scenario here? You guys enter a real relationship where you're barred from ever talking about your real feelings? We all (hopefully) know that the foundation for any good relationship is communication. Period. It is impossible to have a healthy long-term relationship with someone who doesn't know how to communicate.

Oh, and don't even get me started on the idea that you're going to magically one day be able to get them to open up. Take the Human Void at face value and imagine not just a relationship but an entire lifetime with them. Imagine going through a family tragedy with someone who doesn't like to "talk about feelings." Imagine trying to confront your partner of five years about something that's deeply hurting you and having them just walk out because they couldn't handle the conversation.

Escape Plan: First things first, complete the exercise above. Accept that you will not change them. I hope this is enough to convince you that ending things with this guy ASAP is dodging a massive bullet in terms of your future. If it's not, just give it time. Eventually, something is going to bother or upset you, you're going to go to them to talk about it, and they're going to shut you down. I'd rather spare you the pain of getting to that point on your own, but if you need to get there to understand how incapable this person is of maintaining a healthy adult relationship, so be it.

In terms of how to actually end things with this person, try to keep it simple. They're not one for conversations and any sort of big talk you try to have with them is just going to fall on deaf ears. Spare yourself the trouble. Send a text, say something point-blank IRL, or even ghost them. Whatever you do, don't expect a big reaction out of them when you do go ahead and end things.

Signs You're Falling for a Human Void

- ☐ You feel even more nervous than usual bringing up important topics.

- ☐ You have been shut down every time you tried to talk about your feelings.

- ☐ You rarely have conversations that dig deeper than surface level.

- ☐ You can never get a firm "yes" or "no" on plans.

- ☐ You have no idea how they really feel about anything.

- ☐ You are in a constant panic that they're going to ghost you.

- ☐ You feel like you're screaming into the abyss every time you try to confront them.

- ☐ You can go days without hearing from them.

- ☐ You never really have any idea what they're up to.

- ☐ You have wasted at least 10 GB of data on your family plan trying to get your friends to help decode your interactions with them.

EUNICE	YOU
"If I talk at them for long enough, they'll eventually give in and have a real conversation with me."	"This is a colossal waste of my time. I'm out."

THE NICE (ENOUGH) PERSON

Definition: You date the Nice (Enough) Person simply because you can't quite find anything wrong with them. They're *fine*. They get the job done, and they check all of your on-paper boxes. But you don't feel even slightly excited about them. Instead, you're hoping that maybe if you give it enough time you'll *start* getting excited about this very safe option.

IRL Example: Remember Tara from the last chapter? Her ex-husband was a textbook Nice (Enough) Guy.

Why They're a Waste of Your Time: Listen, I get the appeal of this person. As I mentioned earlier, according to the YouGov[6] survey, 39 percent of single women are afraid of getting hurt. Heck, I used to *be* one of those women. Even though I'm in a good, healthy relationship now, I still sometimes feel terrified of getting hurt. So I get why after having had a few train-wreck situationships it can be appealing to settle for someone you're lukewarm about.

But you cannot allow that fear of getting hurt to push you into settling into a relationship you aren't thrilled about. I actually don't believe love always needs to be an immediate fireworks–type situation. My friend Zara Barrie—a great writer you should check out— likes to say real love is oftentimes a "slow burn."[7] And I agree with that. But your reasons for being with someone should always be more of a "why" than a "why not." You are awesome, so you *deserve* to be with someone you're genuinely excited to be with.

Escape Plan: This one can be difficult to get out of because, well, there's nothing necessarily wrong. That being said, there's definitely a little voice in the back of your head that's already warned you that this relationship isn't right. Go with that voice. (And if you're scared of being alone, go back to the last chapter.) You'll be OK. Better than OK! You'll be great.

If that's not convincing enough for you, do it for the poor person you're seeing. They deserve to be with someone who's *excited* about being with them, not someone who actively needs to convince herself of why she's with them. Because this person really did nothing wrong, be as nice as possible. Tell them how great they are, but tell them they deserve better and you do, too. Then move on.

Signs You've Fallen for a Nice (Enough) Person

☐ You feel nothing when you get a text from them.

☐ You're most excited about their on-paper attributes.

☐ You spend a lot of time fantasizing about your ex.

☐ You could easily envision your life without them in it.

☐ You know that you'd dump them if someone better came along.

☐ You can't think of more than a couple of generic adjectives to describe them.

☐ You get irrationally annoyed by totally harmless things they do.

☐ You recently got hurt by someone, and this person feels refreshingly safe.

☐ You feel inexplicably guilty whenever they do something nice for you.

☐ You find yourself regularly having to convince yourself of why you like them.

EUNICE	YOU
"There's no *real* reason to dump them. Might as well stick around."	"My feeling literally nothing toward them is more than enough reason to dump them."

THE BELITTLER

Definition: This person is–simply put–a condescending jerk. They're constantly giving backhanded compliments and making you feel like you're not good enough for one reason or another.

IRL Example: "He would criticize everything, but in a condescending way so it would almost seem nice at first, but then you'd realize it was rude," Elaine, a 32-year-old living in Los Angeles, told me via Instagram DM of her belittling ex. "I was constantly in a state of 'wait, what??' Like, I started working out while we were together and after I'd lost a few pounds he said, 'Oh it's so nice, I can actually fit my arms all the way around you now,' which is not really a compliment considering he could do that the whole time!" Another example? "I'm from the Bay Area, but live in SoCal, but when we were together I'd only been living here a couple years, so I used GPS on my phone to get around a lot and he would say 'awww you don't know how to get anywhere without Google, that's so cute' (meanwhile, he's from SoCal). Just constantly trying to belittle me."

Why They're a Waste of Your Time: Eventually those little digs are going to get to you. And, if you guys aren't even officially dating yet, I'm going to go ahead and guess this is just the beginning. You really think they're going to start going *easier* on you once you're official? No, this person is going to keep chipping away at your self-confidence one dig at a time. You deserve to be with someone who values your opinions and sees you as an equal; not some condescending egomaniac who's constantly trying to put you down.

Escape Plan: If you really like this person and you're set on giving it a shot, you can *try* calling them out for their condescending comments and see if they actually change. I genuinely hope they do! There could really be a chance they don't even realize they're making these insufferable comments.

That being said, there also really could be a chance this is just who they are, in which case you need to tell them you deserve better than someone who thinks it's OK to speak to you like that and move on.

Signs You're Falling for a Belittler

☐ | You always feel dumb around them.

☐ | You don't feel like they're ever really listening to you.

☐ | You never feel like you're good enough for them.

☐ | You find yourself, like Elaine, in that constant state of "Wait, what?"

☐ | You're constantly getting unsolicited advice from them.

☐ | You've been mansplained to by them on multiple occasions.

☐ | You have awkwardly laughed at weird comments they've made because you weren't sure what else to do.

☐ | You feel like their damsel in distress.

☐ You wouldn't repeat some of the stuff they've said to you to your friends and family because you know they'd be furious.

☐ You don't feel like your best self around them.

EUNICE	YOU
after they say something rude "They're right. I suck."	*after they say something rude* "Ew, I don't need this kind of negativity in my life. *Byee.*"

I know firsthand that what I'm asking is way easier said than done. Letting go of some of these situationships can feel near impossible. Some of you might have been stuck seeing some of these tampons for months—maybe even years! It's not going to be easy to cut them out of your life entirely. But, again, keeping them in your life is just a colossal waste of your precious time. They've got to go.

But that doesn't mean you can't be sad about letting them go. Give yourself time to grieve if you're feeling sad. Don't feel like you're not allowed to mourn the loss of the person in your life just because it wasn't a "real relationship." I know what it's like to have to cut ties with someone you were never *really* dating. It sucks. It hurts. The first time I tried to end things with my "He's Perfect, But" guy, I had to call in sick to work the next day because I couldn't stop crying. And on top of feeling devastatingly sad, I felt embarrassed. My Eunice brain was flooded with all sorts of insecure thoughts. *He wasn't even really my boyfriend. How can I be so sad about someone who wasn't even really my boyfriend? This is so embarrassing.* And then, of course, I started doubting my own decision. *Maybe it would have worked out if I waited longer. Maybe he thinks I'm crazy for ending it. Am I crazy? Do I look crazy? Well, I'm currently crying over a boy who wasn't even my boyfriend, so . . .* aaand back to square one.

The best advice I can give you—from personal experience and from watching dozens of friends go through this—is to treat this like a real breakup. Don't be embarrassed. You ended something with someone you cared about. It's going to hurt. So, treat it like a breakup. Go back a chapter and refresh yourself on some tips for handling a breakup. After a while, it will hurt less. Not only will it hurt less, but you'll come out on the other side 1) stronger, and 2) proud of yourself for managing to get out of a relationship that wasn't at all serving you.

EUNICE	YOU
"I can't cry over him! He wasn't even my boyfriend!!!!!!!!!!!!!!!"	"My feelings are real and I'm allowed to be sad over this, so I'm going to take the time to get over it at my own pace."

I hate to bring the toilet metaphor up again—Who I am kidding? No I don't—but think of the actual process of unclogging a toilet. It's by no means fun. It takes way more physical labor than any activity already so inherently gross should ever require. And, even after you've unclogged it, you're oftentimes left with a disgusting mess to clean up. But eventually you finish wiping down your bathroom, you take a shower, you change into clean clothes, and you're officially able to take in a deep breath of fresh, non-stinky air because *finally* the mess is over. And the best part? You were the one who got yourself out of it.

Don't Be a Eunice . . .

- Just cut out the person who's wasting your time, no matter how much it hurts.
- Just treat your brain like a prewar-apartment toilet—no tampons allowed.
- Just take the time to be sad after you end things—whether it's for an hour or for a year.

Reframing Rejection

When it comes to the ability to be vulnerable, there's nobody I admire more than my friend and former coworker Alexia.* While I spent the vast majority of my single life avoiding rejection with the same fervor as a Real Housewife avoiding a nonalcoholic beverage, Alexia has always embraced it. "I have never been scared of rejection and have always been reckless with opening up my heart," she tells me. "I have always been turned inside out, like a raw open wound."

OK, I know being a "raw open wound" doesn't exactly sound enticing, but Alexia swears her love life is better off for it. "I have been able to gather a lot of dating experience because I never shied away from rejection, ever," she explains. "So, I was able to go on more dates and learn more about myself and what I actually want in a partner. Yeah, maybe I get hurt more easily, but that doesn't really scare me or bother me at all. I never fear getting hurt."

---

* Yes, the same Alexia who once followed Worldstar to keep tabs on an ex. See? You can simultaneously be a Eunice and an *icon*.

I've watched firsthand as Alexia unabashedly put herself out there with countless guys. Sometimes, like with her current boyfriend, her approach has rewarded her with love. Other times, her approach left her rejected. Yes, she'd be hurt. But, like a Marvel hero whose superpower is unshakable vulnerability, she'd bounce back yet again fully prepared to put her heart on the line with the next guy.

Even though I've come a *long* way in terms of my own extremely visceral fear of rejection, I still find myself feeling jealous of people like Alexia—people with this innate ability to fearlessly put their hearts on the line time and time again—for two distinct reasons.

First, on a practical level, I'm jealous of how much time they save. I mean, imagine just being able to tell someone how you feel as soon as you start feeling it!! It's such an efficient way to live. Worst case, they say they don't feel the same way and you manage to spare yourself months, if not years, of pining over someone who was never that into you to begin with.

Second, and more important, there's the fact that people like Alexia get to look back on their dating careers without any regrets or what-ifs. They don't find themselves wide awake at two in the morning wondering what would have happened if they'd only told their middle school crush how they felt. They Just Send the Text and move on with their lives regret-free.

EUNICE	YOU
wide awake at 2:00 a.m. on a Tuesday night	*sound asleep at 2:00 a.m. on a Tuesday night*
"What if I had just *told* Taylor how I felt?! Would we be together now?!"	(or at the clurb, whatever floats your boat)

My friend—let's call her Tessa—is a 27-year-old living in San Francisco. When it comes to rejection, putting herself out there didn't always come naturally. Even outside of romantic relationships, she says she cares "a lot" what people think of her. "I need to be liked," she explains. "It's part of who I am as a person, so when it comes to dating, rejection feels like it would be part of my identity. Like, if I was rejected, it would show who I was—that people don't like me."

So, like any self-respecting Eunice, Tessa has spent most of her dating career opting for playing it cool over allowing herself to be vulnerable. "You've got to play it cool, man," she jokes. In addition to proving to her crushes that she's "super, super cool," Tessa says pretending like she didn't actually care about people she had big feelings for was an attempt to psych herself out: "I'm afraid of rejection, so if I tell myself I don't care that much, it makes it seem like if I were to get rejected it would be 'no big because I'm super chill like that.'"

Unfortunately, the whole "playing it cool" tactic, which Tessa admits she swore by for years, left her with nothing but a long list of what-ifs. "If I think back to college me, I tried to play it cool and *played* it cool to the point where I seemed uninterested," she shares, bringing up a guy she was hooking up with during her junior and senior years. "I was trying to be so chill that it actually came off as uninterested and so what I regret is that I wasn't just forthcoming about how I felt." Nowadays, when she looks back on it, Tessa is less concerned with how he would have felt about her and more interested in how she would have personally benefited from having been more vulnerable. "I think I would have learned more about what I needed to do in a relationship," she says, adding that staying so guarded stopped her "from being able to grow as far as understanding dating."

The ironic part is, even as Tessa was bending over backward trying to avoid rejection, she still wound up getting rejected—just not on her own terms. After years of her playing it cool, the guy she was seeing in college started openly seeing other people because he assumed Tessa wouldn't care (you know, because she's so chill). But, of course, Tessa *did* care. "Then you go into creating a narrative of 'What if I had done it differently?' and you realize all of these things you should have done and it's almost this weird alternate twist where you don't believe the rejection," she explains of her thoughts at the time. "You're like 'He doesn't actually know who I am. If I had actually shown who myself was, there's no way that this would have happened.' You beat yourself up when it probably would have just been healthier to accept the rejection."

Now, after years of therapy, she knows that subscribing to the "if he really knew me" narrative was just her way of avoiding actually feeling the sadness that comes along with accepting rejection. But it only wound up leaving her 1) still hurt, and 2) stuck ruminating on what could have been if only she'd shown him the real her. She now realizes the only way to move forward would be to actually allow herself to "feel the sadness" and go on from there.

EUNICE	YOU
"OMG, if they knew the *real* me, they would have never rejected me! Yeah, it's chill. This was just a classic mix-up. It's not like I even care about them anyway, ha-ha."	"Someone I really liked didn't want to be with me and that sucks, so I'm going to let myself be sad, then focus on moving on."

While not every single woman fears rejection in the same way Tessa and I once did, many do. In the survey, YouGov found 29 percent of single women[1] list being rejected as one of the top three dating-related fears that make them the most anxious. In other words, almost a third of single women aren't exactly born with Alexia's innate ability to face rejection head-on.

But, unfortunately for the non-Alexias of the world, embracing rejection is key to Just Sending the Text and thus letting go of dating anxiety. (I mean, *come on*. You had to know by the title of the book alone that what I'm asking us all to do here involves a high risk of rejection.) Just Sending the Text is about refusing to waste any more of our precious time with anyone unless they're the *right* person for us, and part of that process requires us to weed out the ~~idiots~~ people who don't actually want to be with us.

Getting rejected isn't exactly going to make anyone want to jump off the couch and dance around the living room blasting Kool & the Gang's "Celebration." It stings. But the severity of that sting correlates directly to how personally we take the blow. This is a problem considering the fact that, for many, the knee-jerk reaction is to take romantic rejection extremely personally. Because, on a basic human level, we all know that the scariest part of getting rejected isn't the possibility of losing the person rejecting us. No, the *scariest* part of getting rejected is the possibility that the rejection will break us—the idea that this person is going to deem us unworthy and that we're going to believe their assessment.

A 2015 Stanford study[2] found that the emotional damage that results from rejection can last for years for some, even getting in the way of their future relationships. These people aren't struggling for years because they're still hung up on the person who rejected them; they're struggling because they haven't been able to shake the idea that they're not good enough. "Those who see rejections as revealing a core truth about themselves as a person, something about who they *really* are, may be more likely to struggle with recovery and carry rejection with them into the future," the study's lead author, Lauren C. Howe, explained in a 2016 *Stanford News* report[3] detailing her research. According to Howe, these are the same people who look to romantic partners as a "source of information about the self." Essentially, this Stanford study found that there are two types of people when it comes to rejection:

- People who think their personalities are fixed and unchanging and thus take rejection as a sign their personality will forever be lacking something that would have otherwise made them lovable.
- People who think their personalities are capable of growth and change and thus are able to move forward

from rejection without carrying any sort of insecurities into future relationships.

EUNICE	YOU
"He rejected me, just like every other guy. That's it. There's my proof. I'm unlovable."	"Ouch. That hurt. But I'll bounce back from this eventually."

The good news here is that the first group in the study is wrong. *All* of our personalities are capable of growth and change. Take Alexia, for example. While she admittedly used to take her rejections personally, she's changed the way she processes them. "Now I definitely am confident enough to know that it's not about me," she says. "Even if it *is* about me, it's not that there's something wrong with me; it's just that I'm not the person he's looking for and that's not a reflection of me. That's a reflection of him and his needs."

Even Tessa was able to shift her mind-set with time. In fact, it took her getting rejected twice by the same guy to accept being rejected was no indication of her own self-worth. "I had done a lot of work on myself in the years leading up to it." She adds with a laugh that she's done *so* much work on herself that her roommate now refers to her as "Post-Therapy Tessa." It was her experience in therapy that Tessa believes really gave her the confidence to finally step out of her cool-girl comfort zone and allow herself to, for the first time, be vulnerable. "I learned self-worth and what I deserved and in a lot of ways learning that forced me to do better for myself," Tessa says of her experience in therapy.

Part of doing better for herself involved bailing herself out of relationship purgatory with a close friend turned hookup buddy. "It was just like, 'I'm at a point in my life where I don't deserve to be held in limbo, so I just needed an answer.'" And so, she went for it.

She Just Sent the Text. In this case, her "text" was an IRL conversation. They were out together one night, and she asked what they were doing and how he felt and . . . he said he didn't want a relationship. "I went back into [my old pattern of] not really believing him," she recalls. "I was like, 'He's lying. He's just not ready for a relationship,'" (BTW, Tessa isn't the first woman on earth who's done this; like I said earlier, the YouGov survey found 17 percent of women[4] have recently compromised on the type of relationship they were in with hopes that their partner would change with time, with that number jumping to 20 percent for women between the ages of 18 and 34, and to 23 percent for women between the ages of 35 and 54).

On the surface, Tessa was telling herself she was fine because he didn't *actually* mean the rejection. But deep down inside, she says she was beating herself up by buying into the hookup culture lie that tells us admitting we want relationships automatically makes us undesirable. "I went down the path of 'He must think I'm so crazy,'" she says, adding she thinks that path "is the most dangerous spiral of rejection." Now, looking back, she sees things with more clarity. "It's so wild how in those moments you can cause yourself to believe that you're crazy because what did I do that was psychotic? I told someone how I felt about them."

EUNICE	YOU
"OMG, I'd never tell them how I feel. That's *so* weird."	"Weird is actively choosing to keep myself in a state of limbo just to play it cool for this person who doesn't even seem to care about me."

To prevent him from thinking she's "crazy" again and, more important, to change his mind about that not-wanting-a-relationship thing, Tessa kept him around for another year, even staying in close touch with him when he moved across the country. (Again, she's not the first woman on earth to do this—like I said in Step One, 10 percent of women in the YouGov survey[5] said they've recently continued to date someone even after they said that person didn't want a relationship, with that number jumping to 23 percent for women between the ages of 18 and 34). "I held on to that [hope that he'll change his mind] for so long and I got into this cycle of lots of talking, lots of late-night phone calls, visited him in the new city, all of that stuff," she says. But when he came to visit her, something shifted for Tessa. She confronted him again and, when he maintained he still wasn't interested in a relationship, she finally decided to accept the rejection. "I could go for hours analyzing the reasons as to why I'm being rejected . . . because I wanted to not believe it. But, in order to move on, I had to believe the rejection," she says. "Like, this will not go anywhere."

EUNICE	YOU
"Maybe if I stick around for long enough, I'll convince them to change their mind about that whole not-wanting-to-date-me thing."	"Maybe I deserve to date someone who doesn't have to be *convinced* that they want to be with me."

She's also no longer beating herself up over it. "I actually don't take it personally," she says, crediting support from friends and family and another year of learning how to love herself. "I think not taking it personally just comes with more confidence, more self-esteem, and knowing your self-worth," she says. "The most important thing I've ever learned in my whole life is that you have control over how people affect you." For Tessa, she's been setting boundaries with the friend turned hookup buddy by:

- Actively reminding herself that his decision not to be in a relationship with her is no indication of her own self-worth.
- Keeping him in her life as a friend *cautiously*.

About that second part: "This time around with him, when we text—which we have been—I have a different conversation with myself about 'If he hurts you, it's not because he chose to. It's because you let him. You have these answers on how this impacts you and it's now up to me to figure out how I let this in. Like, how much of this do I let impact me?"

EUNICE	YOU
gets a text from guy who rejected her "OMG! He really does love me! I'm *not* an undatable loser after all!"	*gets a text from guy who rejected her* "This means absolutely nothing. I'm just as datable as I was before I got this 'sup' text."

Don't think you can see a text from the person who rejected you *without* placing any extra weight into it? That's fine. Not all of us, myself included, are as great at establishing healthy boundaries as Tessa is. If you feel yourself spiraling every time you see that person's name on your phone screen, do yourself a favor and block them. Even if it's just temporarily.

EUNICE	YOU
feels heart racing at sight of rejector's name on her phone "Oh, I should def respond to this."	*feels heart racing at sight of rejector's name on her phone* *blocks them immediately*

OK, now back to Tessa. Yes, she is handling the rejection swimmingly this time around, but—let me be extra clear here—that doesn't mean she wasn't sad. "Oh God, I cried for, like, three days," she says of getting rejected again. "I think the difference there was that it hurt because it was loss . . . losing a part of your life makes you feel like you have to find something to fill whatever that is and it's sad. But [the second time he told me he doesn't want anything more] there was, like, a sense of 'This is sad. You will be OK. You just have to stick to your guns.'"

No matter how confident or self-aware you are, rejection is always going to make you spiral into a slew of uncomfortable thoughts. It's just up to you to decide whether you want to grow from that spiral or let it destroy you. The way I see it, when it comes to rejection there are two types of spirals:

- The infamous **downward spiral**: I'm not good enough / No one will ever love me / I'm crazy / Maybe if I stick around for long enough, they'll change their mind. . . .
- The wildly underrated **upward spiral**: I'm sad / I'm embarrassed / I'm angry / But this doesn't define me / I'll move on from this. . . .

Don't get me wrong. Neither thought pattern is a blast. But the downward spiral leaves us unable to recover. It gives our rejectors a disproportionate amount of power over our sense of self and leaves us stuck in a Eunice-like state of self-hate, absolutely terrified of getting rejected again. The upward spiral allows us to feel those uncomfortable feelings while still actively reminding ourselves that *we* are the only people responsible for evaluating our own worth. Instead of leaving us stuck, it gives us the chance to grow from the experience and set ourselves up for healthier relationships moving forward.

Of course, for many of us, our brains have been trained to automatically lunge into a downward spiral every time we get rejected.

If that's you, first and foremost, welcome to the club. You're in good company. Second, I'm sorry your brain has been revolting against you. Rejection is already tough enough as it is. You don't need your mind making things even trickier than they need to be.

To help transform tried and not-so-true downward spirals into *upward* spirals, I've laid out five different common types of rejection. For each, I've provided the downward spiral version of the situation and the upward spiral version of the same situation. I'll let you pick which one you prefer (but please for your own sake choose upward).

Scenario 1: You were rejected by a stranger.

The sitch: You shot your shot with a stranger and got turned down.

IRL example: "I told my friends I thought a guy at the bar was cute, so they went over to him (against my wishes), talked to him, and pointed at me," Nicole, a 22-year-old from Chicago, tells me via Instagram DM. "They walked back over to me and say, 'He said he's very flattered, but he has a girlfriend.' I turn around in shame and embarrassment and take one last glance and he shrugs and mouths 'sorry!'"

The Downward Spiral:

What if that guy was just lying about having a girlfriend? / He probably thought I seemed lame or ugly and just didn't want to hurt my feelings by flat-out rejecting me. / Or maybe he did really have a girlfriend because all of the good guys have girlfriends and so I'll be stuck hooking up with mean douchebags until the end of time. / Ugh, why do I even bother? / I am never putting myself out there again. . . .

No matter what the situation, a downward spiral will have any Eunice playing the incident over and over again in her head, using it as a reason to never put herself out there again. Of course, our strong reaction to this rejection has nothing to do with this particular incident. It's a culmination of years and years of built-up insecurities. Things never panned out with our middle school crush, then that last guy we were hooking up with didn't want a relationship, and now *this*. It's the disgusting icing on the already inedible cake.

The Upward Spiral:

I'm pretty embarrassed and that's OK / This was embarrassing / Wow, my face is so hot right now / But eventually this will be less embarrassing and my face will return to a normal temp / I can't wait to laugh about this with my friends tomorrow / Just because this one guy has a girlfriend doesn't mean every good guy has a girlfriend / I still like me and that's all that matters. . . .

Nicole took a similar approach to the above upward spiral when she was rejected, by acknowledging that it was embarrassing in the moment but choosing to laugh about it in the long run. "It was slightly mortifying but mostly a funny story to think back on," she says. Shame has a way of making us feel isolated. Finding a way to laugh about it with friends takes our spiral upward by reminding us:

- We're not alone.
- This isolating experience actually gave us something to connect with our friends over.

EUNICE	YOU
gets rejected by stranger once "That's it. There's my proof. I'm unlovable. I will *never* put myself out there again. This was a huge mistake."	*gets rejected by stranger once* "This stranger's opinion of me means nothing. Just because he wasn't interested doesn't mean the next guy won't be, either. I'm gonna let myself be embarrassed about it in the moment, then laugh about this at brunch with my friends tomorrow."

Scenario 2: You were rejected by *basically* a stranger.

The sitch: You had a first date or a dance floor make-out with someone that you *thought* went well, only to get rejected.

IRL example: My friend Courtney, a 25-year-old living in New York, experienced this rejection via social media with a guy she made out with at a party. "I made out with him at a party super drunk, and later the next week I requested to follow him on Instagram because my friend said he was into me," she says. "I was def into him, and we didn't exchange numbers the night we made out." So, she went ahead and shot him a follow. But things didn't quite pan out. "He accepted my request like a month later and never followed me back," she tells me via Instagram DM, aptly punctuating the update with an eye-roll emoji.

The Downward Spiral:

Was it so lame of me to send that follow request? / Was I a bad kisser? / Did he see my pictures on Instagram and immediately decide I wasn't his type? / Did he think I was easy? / He probably doesn't even remember who I am / How embarrassing / Ugh, I must have done something wrong / Why am I even so upset? / I'm so pathetic. . . .

No matter what our first (and only) encounter was, a downward spiral will have Eunices spending hours and hours replaying it on loop until we come up with some sort of explanation of what we did wrong to lose out on this person. Then we'll dwell on that reason why for years to come and let it keep us from ever fully putting ourselves out there again.

The Upward Spiral:

I'm hurt / Actually, I'm also a little angry / I'm angry this person didn't think I was worthy of a follow back / I'm angry he made me feel irrelevant after we shared something intimate together / So I'm going to let myself be sad and angry for a bit / But, ultimately, I know that this person's assessment of me wasn't accurate / I know I'm worthy of a follow back / I know I'm a fire kisser / I know my social media content is fantastic / And I know the right guy will see all of those things. . . .

Whether we were rejected after a kiss like Courtney or after a first date or after a one-night stand, the new thought pattern in our heads should remind us that, yes, it's OK to be upset even if our encounter with this person was brief. We're losing out not just on the actual person but on the *hope* that maybe this was going to go somewhere. We're allowed to be sad about that. But also, we need to remind ourselves that what this person just gave us was a gift. We're not stuck pining over someone who's trying to decide how they feel about us. No, we've been given the freedom to go forth and find someone who has no trouble recognizing how wonderful we are.

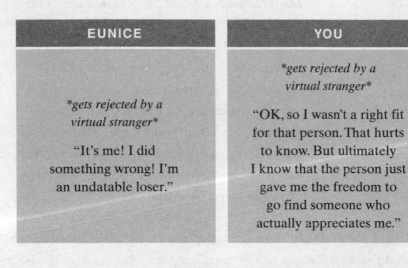

EUNICE	YOU
gets rejected by a virtual stranger "It's me! I did something wrong! I'm an undatable loser."	*gets rejected by a virtual stranger* "OK, so I wasn't a right fit for that person. That hurts to know. But ultimately I know that the person just gave me the freedom to go find someone who actually appreciates me."

Scenario 3: You were rejected by a hookup buddy who didn't want something more.

The sitch: You finally muster up the courage to have the DTR conversation with the person you've been hooking up with and wind up getting shot down.

IRL example: We've already had a few examples of this throughout the book—think Penelope and her ex, Tessa and the friend who rejected her twice, or me and Jack. But let me hit you with a new one. Taylor, 25, was hooking up with an older guy on and off for about three years, who told her he would "never" seriously date someone ten years younger than him. "I thought that I could handle it and I told myself that I didn't want to be with him anyway, but that didn't work," she says with a laugh. "I continued hooking up with him, but I remember vividly walking home after hooking up with him and crying after our hookups." Now she can look back on the situation with a sense of humor, even joking, "He could put his dick inside of me but 'noooo, never date me!'"

The Downward Spiral:

I don't actually even like him that much / Like no, he'll never date me, but who cares?! / I'm chill! / IDGAF / OK, well, maybe I kind of secretly GAF / Maybe if I stick around long enough he'll change his mind and want to date me / He probably does want to date me now but just doesn't fully know it yet / The age thing is probably just masking a fear of commitment stemming from his last relationship / He obviously likes me / He sleeps with me. . . .

When going on a downward spiral after a situation like Taylor's, we might as well rename ourselves "Cleopatra" because we're about to become Queens of DA NILE (lol, get it, like "denial"?!). We'll keep ourselves trapped in a miserable situation by convincing ourselves that everything's fine and we've got this when we most definitely are not fine and we absolutely do not have this. Of course, every situation isn't exactly the same as Taylor's. But every Eunice-like downward spiral we plummet into when we're rejected by hookup buddies is essentially the same delusional attempt at convincing ourselves that:

- We'll be able to change their minds.
- We don't actually care *that* much.

The Upward Spiral:

I need to walk away from this / He told me he doesn't want a relationship / I want a relationship / Those are the facts / I deserve better / I'm going to be sad / I'm going to have to mourn this like a real breakup / I might even have to block his number for a while / But eventually maybe I'll look back on this without my heart feeling like it's about to explode. . . .

The key to healthily getting over this kind of rejection is to first and foremost, like Tessa said, believe them when they say they don't want what we do. This process will obvi be sad. And that's OK. Please, please, please—I'm begging you. Let yourself be sad. We deserve to treat these rejections like real breakups. We deserve to cry into a pint of Ben & Jerry's and talk about it for way too long with our friends. That's the only chance we have at being able to laugh about it later. Like I said earlier, laughter has the power to take what we once saw as shameful and isolating and turn it into something that brings us joy and helps us connect with other people. But that's only true if we're not using it to mask the pain. Feel your feelings, *then* laugh.

EUNICE	YOU
guy she wants to be official with says he doesn't want to be official	*guy she wants to be official with says he doesn't want to be official*
"Oh, ha-ha. Totally chill! I'm fine. No, I'm not crying. These are just allergies. We're fine. We're good. See you tomorrow night? Yeah, cool. It's casual."	"OK, well. We clearly want different things, so we should stop doing whatever this has been. This is going to hurt, but I'd rather be hurt on my own than anxious trying to come up with new ways to con you into wanting to date me."

Scenario 4: You were rejected by someone you weren't even that into.

The sitch: You've been keeping this person around as a distraction, a backup plan, and/or a confidence boost when suddenly, out of the blue, *they* end things with *you*.

IRL example: "I started seeing this guy, but I wasn't over my ex," says a 20-year-old woman from Boston—let's call her Christa—of a situation that took place two years prior. "And my ex decided he wanted to meet up, so I ended things with the new guy to go talk with my ex, who then ghosted me. And I tried to go back to the guy I wasn't really interested in and he said that he was actually glad I had ended things because he wasn't feeling it, either."

The Downward Spiral:

How dare he end things with me? / If I can't get this stupid guy to like me, how will I ever get any guy to like me? / Maybe I had it all wrong / Maybe he was The One all along / Maybe I blew my shot with the one person who would have ever loved me. . . .

No matter what the details, a downward spiral after being rejected by our backup plan is going to leave us questioning our own self-worth. We'll question whether or not we had things wrong all along: *Maybe he really *was* The One?* We'll question if we'll ever get anybody to love us: *If I'm not good enough for him, will I be good enough for anybody?* And we'll question how we could possibly have managed to let this person slip: *If I can't get him, how will I ever get anyone?* The fact that we once upon a time never even liked this person is, of course, no longer even remotely relevant. Now we're fully operating under a new narrative in which they're the one who got away, and we're the worthless loser who lost out.

The Upward Spiral:

Well, this is definitely kind of an ego bruise / But, hey, I have to admit the irony here / Plus, I never liked this guy / And he didn't like me / Isn't that as fair as it gets? / Don't we both deserve to be able to be with people we're excited about? / There was no point in keeping him around anyway / I'm capable of giving myself all of the confidence I was counting on him for. . . .

The important thing to remember here, no matter what the exact circumstance, is that you didn't even like this person. In fact, this could be a great opportunity to explore why you were even keeping them around. What void were they filling, and how can you focus on filling it for yourself? More important, if you're feeling a little upset, as always, let yourself feel that feeling and then, if possible, laugh about it. That's what Christa did, while also maintaining a realistic perspective on the situation. "I was like, 'Damn . . . ,' but at the same time I kind of thought I deserved it and found it humorous," she says. Again, feeling our feelings is key, but, if you're able to find humor in any aspect of this situation, let yourself laugh.

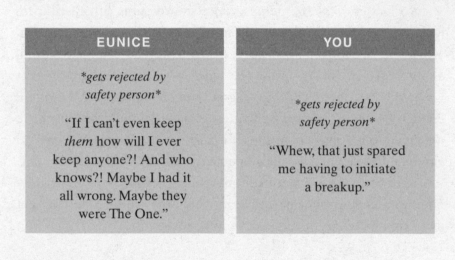

EUNICE	YOU
gets rejected by safety person "If I can't even keep *them* how will I ever keep anyone?! And who knows?! Maybe I had it all wrong. Maybe they were The One."	*gets rejected by safety person* "Whew, that just spared me having to initiate a breakup."

Scenario 5: You were rejected by a longtime love.

The sitch: You were in a very serious relationship and got blindsided with a breakup.

IRL example: "We knew we weren't quite on the same page about kids (he wanted them sooner rather than later whereas I have always been ambivalent), but I thought we would be able to work things out since we did really love each other and really had no issues besides that," a 29-year-old woman from Los Angeles—who I'll call Jenny— tells me via Instagram DM. "We'd been talking about kids a little more seriously in the months before the breakup—but with the assumption that we'd be together, not like deciding if we could move forward. But unbeknownst to me, he at some point decided it wasn't going to work out and broke up with me." Then he got engaged to someone else soon after.

The Downward Spiral:

He got to know the real me and decided I wasn't good enough / Something is inherently wrong with me / What, am I supposed to waste another few years of my life in a relationship only to get dumped again? / If he didn't love me, no one will / I'm unlovable / This pain is never going to end / I'm going to be a depressed, lonely spinster forever / I'll never meet anyone again / Even if I do meet someone again, I won't be good enough. . . .

It's natural to take a breakup like this personally, but a downward spiral makes us take it *extra* personally, doing detective work trying to figure out what's wrong with us. We wind up believing that growing from something this devastating is impossible, and we take the rejection to mean that there's something about the very core of who we are that makes us unlovable.

The Upward Spiral:

This hurts / This really, really hurts / My heart feels like it's split in half / It feels like this pain will never go away / But I know it will / Sometimes I can't help but wonder if I wasn't good enough / But then I remember this was for the best / We were two people who tried to make it work, but ultimately we weren't compatible / That doesn't mean I won't be compatible with the next person / And that doesn't mean what I had with my ex wasn't special. . . .

This spiral is always going to be the saddest. And that's OK. What you're going through is devastating. But it is so important to remember that this isn't a reflection of who you are. Yes, those self-doubting thoughts may float into your head from time to time. But the upward spiral involves you actively shutting those doubts down and reminding yourself this split was bigger than both of you. Take Jenny, for example. "I hadn't experienced a breakup like that before," she says. "So, I've definitely had the thought that he just didn't want me enough to figure things out." That being said, she says the thought only crossed her mind from time to time and that she knew the baby thing was something they would have never been able to compromise on. "We were just on separate paths in life."

EUNICE	YOU
gets dumped by longtime love	*gets dumped by longtime love*
"They got to know me and decided I'm unlovable. And they're right."	"This hurts. And it's probably going to hurt for a long time. But we just weren't compatible."

So, these five situations are all well and good, but what if none of them applies to you because you're so deeply terrified of getting rejected that you've never even bothered to put yourself out there? Well, then I'm going to end this chapter by begging you to take one step out of your romantic comfort zone. If you've been holding back on telling your hookup buddy you want something more, tell them. If you look up from this book and spot someone semi-attractive in your general vicinity, strike up a conversation with them.

If all of the above sounds just way too terrifying to you, start even smaller by joining dating apps. Julia, a 31-year-old living in New York, credits the apps for helping her overcome her fear of rejection. "I think that dating apps help you get over the fear of rejection because there's just so many people," she says. "So, you're talking to multiple people at once. OK, you stop talking to one, but there's ten more in ten seconds." Specifically, she says apps like Bumble that force her to make the first move have made her feel way more confident with putting herself out there.

Similarly, Tessa agrees the apps helped build up her tolerance for rejection before she mustered up the courage to put herself out there with the friend turned hookup buddy. "I was someone who never put themselves out there dating. . . . I avoided it because I was so afraid of how it was going to harm my self-worth and my self-esteem because that was something that I just struggled with in general, so giving someone else the rights and permission to have an impact on my self-esteem felt so scary," she says. "So, as someone who avoided rejection to such an extreme degree, for me going on the apps was like anything in psychology, when you work your muscle and you get more experience and you have more evidence in your evidence bag of like, 'OK, I did this and nothing bad happened.'" Dating apps are a great way to do exactly what Tessa described—to prove to yourself in a low-stakes way that you can get rejected and live to tell the tale.

EUNICE	YOU
"I'm terrified of rejection, so I'm going to avoid it at all costs."	"I'm terrified of rejection, so I'm going to face the fear and overcome it."

Another cool thing about the apps? They let you get a glimpse from the point of view of the rejector. Tessa says, after having been the one to not swipe right or not text back after a so-so Hinge date, she's realized it's possible to reject someone without having any negative feelings toward them as a person. They could be really great, and you could just not be that into it. "It's like, 'I rejected this person, but it's not that I thought they were bad. It's just that I wasn't interested,'" Tessa says of her new mind-set. Obvi this proves that when *you* get rejected, it's possible the person who rejected you felt the same way. There was nothing wrong with you. They just weren't feeling it. And that's OK.

Like it or not, rejection is part of life. Embracing it is going to help you not just in your dating life but in your life as a whole. There is just no way you're going to get yourself the sort of life you deserve if you're not willing to risk rejection. So, do yourself a favor and go get rejected.

Don't Be a Eunice . . .

- Just let yourself be vulnerable.
- Just believe them when they say they don't want to be with you.
- Just embrace the pain, then laugh it off.

Accepting That the Right Person Likes You

One day, about a year after I graduated from college, my friend Kevin unintentionally changed my life, by giving me the best piece of advice I've ever gotten from anyone. I had just moved to New York a few months prior and I really, *really* liked this new guy. He was my "He's Perfect, But" guy—remember him? We called him Paul. OK, well, here's the backstory: Paul and I met at a bar and, even though he didn't live in New York, we had spoken every day since then. For months, we'd text each other good morning and good night and fill all the hours in between with inside jokes and stories about our weirdly similar upbringings. We did manage to plan a few trips to see each other IRL, but the bulk of our "relationship" was texts.

So, when one day I hadn't heard from him by around lunchtime-ish, I could feel myself plummeting down into Euniceville. Texting was all we had! And now he wasn't texting me! By the time I was walking to grab lunch with Kevin, I was in full panic mode. *Should I text him? Should I wait for him to text me? If I don't text him what if we never talk again? If I do text him what do I even say?! Does he not like me anymore? Is this my proof?* I asked Kevin these questions on loop for fifteen minutes straight, until finally he hit me with this: "Why would you even waste your energy worrying about someone who would maybe never speak to you again?" *Oh, that's a good point.*

I don't think Kevin meant to give me life-changing advice. But he did because what he was saying was relevant far beyond whether or not I should have texted Paul that day. It applied to the entire way I had approached dating up until then. I had been putting all of this effort into thinking about how I should react when the guy I liked inevitably did something to prove that he didn't like me as much as I liked him. My mind was constantly working on overdrive trying to:

- Figure out when things were going to come crashing down with the person I liked.
- Figure out clever ways to *stop* that crash from happening.
- Make sure I was "prepared" for when the crash happened despite my efforts.

But Kevin's offhanded piece of advice forced me to come to terms with a concept I'd refused to consider until that point: Maybe the worst-case scenario didn't really matter as much as I thought it did. I mean, if he *really* was never going to text me back, then he was never worth my time in the first place, right?

As I hope you've gathered by this point, dating with confidence doesn't come naturally to me. But anytime I felt myself getting Eunice-y after this moment, I would stop myself and ask, *If I knew he really liked me, would I still be worrying about this?* The answer is always no. I wouldn't be worried that he hadn't texted me for a few hours if I *knew* he liked me. I wouldn't be worried that he might have misinterpreted that thing I said at dinner last night if I *knew* he liked me. And, if he's worth my time, he does like me. Instead of exhausting myself searching for any and all clues the guys I liked didn't like me back, I started taking comfort in the idea that the right people will stick around, and the wrong ones will weed themselves out.

EUNICE	YOU
catches feelings	*catches feelings*
"Please, God. *Please* let them like me back."	"If they're right for me, they'll like me back."

The problem for many of us, as Ann pointed out in Step Two, is that we're stressing about how the other person feels about us before we've even taken a second to determine how *we* feel about *them*. So, before we even proceed with this chapter, let's take a second for a much-needed pulse check. Before you let your heart rate spike over this person, try asking yourself if you even really like them. More specifically, I'd recommend honestly answering the following questions for yourself:

- Do you feel really, truly, can't-stop-smiling happy when you're around them?
- Do they bring something special to your life that no other person could?
- Are you more excited about them specifically than you are about receiving romantic attention from someone?

If you answer "no" to the above questions, odds are you don't even really like this person that much. So why are you still hurt by them? Well, we all want to be liked. We all crave companionship. And this person was a shot at feeling liked and less alone. It's natural to want their approval. But remember that, while it is absolutely a bruise to the ego, parting ways with someone you didn't even really like is for the better. If the person does wind up rejecting you, they're gifting you the freedom to find someone who makes you really, truly happy. Conversely, if this person hasn't rejected you yet and you've determined you're not feeling it, I'd recommend you get ahead of it now and reject *them*. Don't waste your time trying to win the heart of someone you're not even really interested in. It's not fair to you and it's not fair to them.

OK, now that we've covered that, let's talk about how to proceed when we *do* decide we really like the other person. So many of us waste so much of our time being on high alert for any and all signs that the person we like doesn't like us back. And where does that process ever really get us? More often than not, it leaves us:

- With no real intel.
- Totally stressed and upset the entire time we're seeing them.

Even if you're convinced the person you're seeing really *doesn't* like you back, try operating as though they do. Do it for your own mental health. Don't waste an ounce of your precious energy trying to play what I call the "Do They Like Me" Game. Almost every Eunice-like behavior stems from this gigantic fear that the person we like doesn't like us back. We catch feelings and, suddenly, all of our mental energy goes toward figuring out whether or not the other person is harboring those same feelings for us. Take 21-year-old Austin native Hannah, for example. "I FREQUENTLY check their Venmo history," she tells me of her crush via Instagram DM. "The few times I've found anything, it's just given me more info on if they're talking to more people. It helps me understand if they're interested in more before I'm ready to have that conversation." What she finds has a direct effect on her mood. "If I see something suspicious then I get anxious and, if I see nothing, then I feel better!"

I know exactly what Hannah means because I've been Hannah a million times over. And there's a chance you know what it's like, too, considering that 19 percent of the women in the YouGov survey[1] listed never knowing where they stand with a partner as one of the top three factors in dating that make them anxious, with that number jumping to 23 percent for women between the ages of 18 and 34. We have no idea how the person we're seeing feels about us, and that uncertainty freaks us out. So, as a result, we try to quell that anxiety by trying to gather any intel we can about how they feel.

But what if, instead of trying out a side hustle as an amateur detective, we combated our fear of the unknown by shifting the narrative in our heads? In other words, next time you feel the inevitable urge to type their name into your Instagram search bar to see why they haven't responded to your text, remind yourself that **anyone who's _worthy_ of dating you worships the ground you walk on and anyone else is irrelevant**. And, um, I'm sorry but why would you bother wasting your energy trying to social stalk someone irrelevant?

EUNICE	YOU
hasn't heard from crush in two hours	*hasn't heard from crush in two hours*
"Well, maybe I should check to see if they've been on Instagram. Yep, they've been on Instagram. That's it. They're ghosting me. We're over."	"Maybe I should check Insta— Nope! Not going down that rabbit hole. If they like me, I'll hear from them, and if they don't, they don't matter. No extra effort necessary on my end."
cue the Adele and shut the lights	

My main issue with the "Do They Like Me Game" is that when most of us are playing, we aren't necessarily looking for signs that they _do_ like us. For example, like I told you in the first chapter, the YouGov survey found 30 percent of women[2] are looking for signs the person they're seeing is lying or hiding something when they stalk them on social media. We're trying to "prepare" ourselves for the possibility that they might hurt us down the line, but all we really wind up doing is hurting ourselves prematurely.

Which brings me to a concept called "negativity bias." Never heard of it? Neither had I until I watched a TEDx Talk by an Irish psychologist named Jodie Rogers.[3] In her talk, Rogers says human beings have negativity bias, which means "we are preprogrammed to pay more attention to the negative things in life than the positive things in life." This is true in all realms of our lives, from when our boss asks to see us and we start running through the five thousand possible reasons why she could be firing us to when our crush doesn't call after a first date and we start going through the five thousand possible reasons why we blew the date. According to Rogers, the negativity bias is an evolutionary adaptation. As humans, our brains are wired to focus on the negative because, back in the day, we had to be on higher alert for a tiger potentially coming to kill us than we did for the delicious batch of berries growing around the corner. Now, thousands of years later, our brains are still wired to think they need to be hyper-focused on the negative in order to keep us alive.

To a certain extent, that negativity bias still serves us. Our world today isn't immune from life-threatening situations, and it's probably best that we're aware of them. But, for the most part, our love lives don't fall under the umbrella of "life-threatening situations." No matter how hard our brains try to convince us otherwise, not hearing back from our crushes or getting rejected by our hookup buddies or the countless other little things that come up in our dating lives will not kill us. In other words, when it comes to our love lives it's time we start training our brains to notice the berries again.

Whether or not you end up with the person you're seeing in the long run, the overall hope of the Just Send the Text method is to make the time you spend with them more enjoyable. If you spend six months casually dating someone, the goal is to make sure you feel calm and happy during those six months. At the very least, this person shouldn't be adding any extra stress to your life. Your life is just quite simply way too precious to give someone the power to turn it into shambles simply because you like them. And there's no quicker way to turn your life, and whatever maybe-relationship you were about to enter, into shambles than choosing to go on a hunt for signs that the person you're interested in doesn't like you back. Because, let's face it, if you're searching for signs that they don't like you, you will *always* find something.

EUNICE	YOU
receives a "hey" text from crush	
"OMG, they didn't even have the energy to include a question. They hate me. Yeah, they initiated this conversation, but they clearly don't want to keep it going because they *hate* me."	*receives a "hey" text from crush* *is happy to get text from crush*

For the zillionth time, I'm going to repeat: This isn't a book about getting the guy. But which of the two above people do you think has a better shot at having things work out? Anyone who's been a Eunice knows how the rest of her story goes. She freaks out, and then she can't really be herself around her crush because she's convinced that they don't even like her. Then things fizzle out, and she's not sure if it fizzled out because she was right and they never really liked her or because she got weird when she started assuming that they never really liked her.

On the flip side, by Just Sending the Text *you* are giving this a real shot. You're hyper-aware of the signs that this person does like you and this awareness makes you more comfortable and confident around them. Things may work out, and if they do, they'll work out without any major drama. Even if they don't work out, you can look back on the experience and know:

- The person they got to know was the *real* you. There was nothing you could have done differently. Like Ann said back in Step Two, you guys just didn't vibe.
- You enjoyed the time you did have with them, instead of making it unnecessarily miserable for yourself.

But, of course, going down the latter road is way easier said than done. I mean, *duh*. Our brains are naturally prone to go down that Eunice-like path. Undoing the way our brains have been wired for *centuries* isn't going to be easy.

So, next time you feel like indulging yourself in another lose-lose round of the "Do They Like Me Game," come back to this chapter. I'm here to help. Below, I have the major variations of the "Do They Like Me" Game listed. Read along and resolve to *never* play again.

The "I'm Going to Stalk Them on Social Until I Find My Proof" Game

The Game: Ah, an old classic. You're going to scavenge social media for any clues you can possibly find as to whether or not this person likes you—don't act like you're above it; 66 percent of women in the YouGov survey have stalked their crushes on social media for one reason or another. More specifically, 27 percent said they turned to their crush's social media profiles and posts for "support" at the beginning of a relationship.[4]

IRL Example: "My crush and I followed each other on Insta and I was looking at who viewed my Instagram stories and his name was popping up at the top of the 'people who watched your story' list at a lot of the stories," Nicole, the 22-year-old from Chicago who was laughing about being rejected by the guy with the girlfriend in the last chapter, tells me. "My brain: OMG, does this mean he looks at my profile a lot??? I bet it does. OR wait . . . does it mean I look at his profile a lot? Or is it just because he recently followed? To this day, I have no idea which option it is."

Five Reasons Why You Think You Should Play

- To see if they've been on social media, even though they haven't texted you.
- To see if they've seen your story.
- To see if they've liked your latest post.
- To see if they're still in contact with their ex.
- To see if they've followed anyone shady.

Five Reasons Why You Actually Shouldn't Play

- None of the information that you see on social media will actually give you any real intel (think: Penelope wasting months of her life stalking her ex for answers, only to find nothing).
- We all know this isn't going to be quick—a "quick" check of their profile is going to send you down a half-hour-long rabbit hole ending on, like, their mom's best friend Susan's Venmo account.
- Let's say you *do* find what you believe to be hard proof that they're not into you. Congrats, you just went out of your way to break your own heart. (That is, until they send you a text and immediately wipe your brain clean of any evidence you found.)
- The amount of irrelevant personal information you're about to dig up on them is only going to leave you feeling unnecessarily creepy and insecure next time you guys hang out.
- The best-case scenario is that you find some small semblance of hope that they *do* like you—maybe they

watched your story! Maybe they liked your picture! But, more often than not, those positive signs are just as arbitrary as the negative ones. I mean, think about how many people's pictures you absentmindedly like on Instagram.

What You Should Do Instead

Delete social media from your phone and go distract yourself with something else like bingeing a new show on Netflix or reading a book or FaceTiming your mom. Speaking of your mom, if you *do* insist on going on social media, try stalking someone like her instead. In other words, play some soothing music and calm yourself down by looking through pictures of someone who you *know* loves you—like your mom or your best friend.

EUNICE	YOU
hasn't heard from crush in twenty-four hours	*hasn't heard from crush in twenty-four hours*
"Let me check Instagram real quick just to see if they've been on."	"I guess now's as good a time as any to start *Breaking Bad*."
six hours later	*six hours later*
"Whoa, I can't believe their mom's best friend, Susan, still pays her ex-stepson's rent every month."	"OK, I get the hype. Next episode, please and thank you."

The "I'm Going to Dissect Our Every Interaction We've Had with My Bestie" Game

The Game: You sit down with your friends and go through every clue you've gathered thus far about how your crush feels about you; this is another pretty common game, as 24 percent of single women in the YouGov survey say they've described their crush's behavior to a friend in order to have them help determine whether or not a crush likes them and 19 percent of single women say they've done the same to two or more friends.*

IRL Example: I'm a sucker for Heads Up! but it's safe to say no game could even remotely compare to the love I once upon a time had for the "I'm Going to Dissect Our Every Interaction We've Had with My Bestie" game. If one of my closest friends growing up, Annie, and I spent as much time studying after school as we did on the phone dissecting every single interaction we had with our crushes in high school, we'd both have Harvard degrees by now. Here's how a sample round of this game would go: Annie would describe to me, in detail, something her crush said that day, usually something as simple as "You're my best girl friend." Then, we would spend *hours* deciding exactly what that meant. *Is he friend-zoning you? Is he in love with you? Did he really mean "girlfriend," one word? Who were these other girlfriends he was alluding to? Honestly, what a jerk. But isn't that what you love about him? The fact that he's kind of a jerk? It's not really that he's a jerk, is it? It's more that he's so honest....* Sometimes the dissection would get so intense that we'd have to hang up the phone and drive to each other's houses for an emergency school-night sleepover to continue the conversation IRL.

---

* For women between the ages of 18 and 34, those numbers jumped to 34 percent and 28 percent, respectively.

Five Reasons Why You Think You Should Play

- To get an outside opinion on the thoughts playing on infinite loop in your head. You think that this is you being *rational*.
- To get a confidence boost from your friend. Think: "Of course they like you!!!"
- To get a reality check from a different friend. Think: "They're just not that into you."
- To get some insight into the depths of your crush's psyche.
- To get some intel on if you did anything to make them no longer like you.

Five Reasons Why You Actually Shouldn't Play

- The only person who has any real input on how your crush feels is . . . drumroll, please . . . your crush. Your friend's intel is no better than your own.
- Telling your friend about every sign your crush doesn't like you might come around to bite you in the butt if things do pan out between you guys. (For example, Nina regrets the way her now boyfriend came off to her friends when they were first hooking up. "It sucked because in my case he really was a great guy and had never actually done anything wrong—but my friends only knew the pain I had been through crying over him," she explains. "To them it seemed like he really had hurt me, when in reality I was crying over my own anxiety about him not liking me.")
- If your friend decides they're not into you and you're wasting your time, but you keep seeing them, then you've just created an extremely awkward situation.

- Whatever you decide in your long-drawn-out analysis with your friend is going to alter the way you act around your crush next time you see them.
- Spending hours trying to decode these (usually meaningless) clues with your friends is only going to wind up making them an even bigger deal than they were before in your mind.

What You Should Do Instead

I'm all for getting your thoughts out there, so by all means *vent* to your friends. Tell them how you're feeling and keep them in the loop of what's going on. But just make sure to:

- Be cognizant of the picture you're painting of your crush—make sure you're evenly talking about both the good and the bad.
- Don't expect your friends to be your window into your crush's mind.

EUNICE	YOU
talking to bestie	*talking to bestie*
"OK, so he told me he's 'not looking for a relationship right now.' What do you think that means? Does he really not want a relationship or was that just an excuse because he doesn't like me? Do you think this is because of his parents' divorce? I think he was really traumatized by that. What do you think??!"	"He told me he's not looking for a relationship right now and I'm super bummed about it because I definitely wanted a relationship with him. I know he's busy with work, but when this stuff happens I can't help but take it personally."

The "I'm Going to Dissect Every Interaction We've Had in My Head" Game

The Game: For most of us Eunices, engaging in a round of this game feels involuntary. We catch feelings and our minds become flooded with replays of our last encounters with our crush. We obvi then over-analyze them to try to pinpoint exactly what we did to drop the ball during said encounter.

IRL Example: The 24-year-old woman behind the @datinginalabama Instagram account admitted to me that she went so far as to once possibly break the law to get some insight on how her crush really felt. "I think this is illegal, but I voice recorded forty mins of a date because I wanted to see how I responded, and how he responded to questions," she admits.

Five Reasons Why You Think You Should Play

- To get clarity on what you did wrong, so you don't make that mistake again.
- To remind yourself of (totally insignificant) moments you overlooked to convince yourself there have always been signs they didn't like you.
- To punish yourself by replaying that one embarrassing thing you did over and over.
- To create an ongoing tally for yourself of all the signs they don't like you.
- To keep your hopes as low as possible, ensuring you won't be surprised if things go south.

Five Reasons Why You Actually Shouldn't Play

- It is pretty much mental torture.
- You're going to lose sleep.
- You're going to lose focus at work, with your friends, and in pretty much every other realm of life.
- The human memory isn't even that accurate, so most of the scenes you're replaying in your head aren't quite real.
- You're going to psych yourself out to the point of no return and it's going to affect your relationship with your crush moving forward.

What You Should Do Instead

It's not easy to opt out of this game. Sometimes it feels like our brains can't help but plummet into this rabbit hole as soon as we catch feelings. So instead of trying to push the thoughts away, try writing them down. Release all of the toxic thoughts from your head by writing them all out, then throw out the paper you wrote them on. Once you've thrown that paper out, try shifting your thoughts to the positive by forcing yourself to write out all of the signs they *do* like you and all of the signs you *are* doing something right. Keep that paper and read it next time you're feeling like playing.

EUNICE	YOU
"I suck. I suck. I suck. Let me play all of the reasons why I suck and why they don't like me on loop in my mind on repeat forever."	"I *feel* like I suck, but I logically know that's not true. So, I'm going to write out all my crazy thoughts, throw them away, then force myself to write out a new, happier narrative."

If the need to know what's going on is truly gnawing at you to the point of no return, set yourself free by Just Sending the Text. Tell them how you feel and ask them what the deal is between you guys (more on how to do that in Step Seven). They are the only one who will give you any sort of *real* insight into what's going through their head. Every other amateur investigation you attempt is just an anxiety-inducing waste of your own time.

Don't Be a Eunice . . .

- Just shut down any and all ongoing investigations you have with the hopes of finding out how they feel about you.
- Just try looking for signs they *do* like you.
- Just ask them what's going on when the curiosity is just too much to bear.

Be Yourself
(No, Really)

L et me paint you a picture. It's 2:00 p.m. on a Friday afternoon. You're technically *supposed* to be working, but you haven't managed to get anything done because all you can think about is the fact that you went on a great first date two nights ago and you still haven't heard from them. You're ignoring my advice from the last chapter and pouring your energy into exploring all of the possible reasons behind their disappearance. (Did you say something weird on the date? Was the dress you wore unflattering? Did they get hit by a bus?!) Just as you're about to start spiraling, you get a text from them: "Hey. Had a great time with you on Wednesday. Let's do it again sometime soon?" You are over the moon. You're so excited you could leap on top of your desk and start doing the "Cha Cha Slide" right there on the spot.

After spending thirty seconds staring at the text trying to suppress the giant smile that is desperately threatening to break across your face, you excitedly screenshot it and send it to your best friends. Now it's time to get to work—not on your *actual* work, but on crafting a response (duh). You open up the Notes app in your phone because you don't want your crush to see you're typing and draft three different options:

- "Hey! Same here. I'm free next Thursday?"
- "Hey, stranger ... I'm busy next week, maybe the week after?"
- "Hii, good to hear from you! My friend's actually having a party tomorrow if you want to drop by."

You text all three options to your friends, and after much debate, it's decided: Option 1 is the winner. But, of course, you don't Just *Send* the Text right then and there! It's only been fifteen minutes since they texted you! You need to play it cool, obvs. So, instead, you save Option 1 in your notes and spend the rest of your workday counting down the hours until it becomes socially acceptable to reply.

TL;DR—you just effectively wasted a day of your life stressing over playing The Game and will likely blow many more days the same way until you either fizzle out or become official with this person. When I'm referring to "The Game," I am, of course, not referring to the G-Unit rapper behind all of the songs I grinded to in middle school. No, I'm referring to the widely held belief that we essentially have to con people into liking us. While the last chapter talked about the "Do They Like Me" games we play to find out how our crushes feel about us, *this* chapter is going to focus on The Game, aka all the hoops we've been taught to jump through in order to make our crushes like us back.

Play it cool! Make them jealous! Pretend to like what they like! Don't be crazy! Don't be creepy! Don't be dramatic! But also, don't be boring! Human beings have been flooded with this idea that there are certain motions we have to go through in order to get people to like us. And, to a certain extent, we all dutifully agree to abide by these unwritten rules.

"I truly think if you say you're not playing The Game, you're lying! You might not be playing The Game in a sense of waiting to respond to make them wonder if you like them, but nobody is going on a first date with no makeup and bad breath being like, 'This is the real me,'" my friend Amber, a 27-year-old living in Chicago, tells me. "It would be like going on a job interview telling the boss, 'Sometimes when I work from home, I'm just watching Netflix with a face mask on shaking the mouse to appear online.' You're playing a game with how quickly you let someone know all the parts of you, in a way. It's all about timing that right, and every girl I know would agree you can't come on too strong, can't talk about exes on the first date, etc. And in my opinion, that's all The Game."

When I started doing research for this chapter, I talked to lots of people with takes similar to Amber's, and I agree with them. On some level, most of us do play The Game. And that's not necessarily a bad thing! If you look at The Game more like a set of general guidelines and less like a set of tenets you need to live and die by, it can even be sweet. Trying to dress up in your favorite outfit for your first date and maybe pop a breath mint beforehand is just *nice*. It proves you like the person enough to make an effort.

Moreover, holding certain things back in the earlier stages helps keep us emotionally safe. For example, we may *feel* like we love someone on the first date, but **that feeling is not fact**. No, seriously. In April 2019 I wrote an article for *Cosmopolitan* called "Is Love at First Sight Even Real? Experts Say Probably Not"[1] and, um, the title pretty much sums it up perfectly. According to psychologists, love at first sight is not a thing. You can have a good feeling at first sight and then eventually fall in love. But in that moment what you're feeling is chemistry—*not* love. Sorry.

So, if The Game is urging you to take your time to make sure you're really into someone before professing your love, then great! I'm all for it. I'm also all for it when it serves as a reminder that we should be focused on our own lives, rather than dropping everything on the spot to go be with our crushes.

But The Game starts to become problematic when it transitions from "Ooh, fun! I'm going to get dressed up for my date" to "I have to put all of my effort into stopping my natural impulses because apparently being myself isn't good enough to find me love." Think about that example at the beginning of this chapter. I'm going to venture to guess most of us have lived through some sort of variation of that emotional roller coaster of a day. But you don't have to live through another one. There are two anti-Game things that you could do in that scenario to make your life infinitely easier:

- Text them first: Of course, don't do this if you have no urge to do it. But if you're a forward person who wishes you could just text them, then forget the stupid rules and text them first. In doing so, you'll have effectively spared yourself the stressful two days of wondering if you'll ever hear from them. And whether they're into you or not, you'll get your answer and I *promise* you that answer won't have anything to do with the fact that you texted them first.

- Respond when you're ready to: If you're just . . . waiting because you feel like it's what you *should* be doing, pause and remind yourself how silly that is. This may sound absolutely wild, but what if you just wrote what you felt like writing, sent it whenever you were ready to send it, and in doing so spared yourself the hours of time wasted? Revolutionary, I know.

EUNICE	YOU
receives text from crush	
celebrates its receipt like a quarterback celebrating the winning touchdown, comes up with response possibilities in notes, consults responses with friends, and sets a reminder on phone to send it in four hours (as if she won't be staring at the clock the entire time anyway)	*receives texts from crush* *quickly writes a response, sends it, and moves on with day*

I despise—yes, despise—The Game when it makes us feel like we have to censor ourselves in order to find love. For example, take Riddhi, a 30-year-old from Austin who often finds herself feeling like she has to hide her blunt nature to get the guy. "A lot of times even if I've been seeing someone for several months, I do feel like I'll come off as too aggressive when I confront things at the time they happen, which leads to me often bottling it up, then just blatantly ignoring red flags altogether until it becomes a toxic mess and the relationship burns down along with my confidence in dating," she tells me via Instagram DM. "Overall, I don't feel like I play the game well, but sometimes I feel like I have to so as not to scare someone off. Those first few months are so odd to me when you first meet someone, and I often feel like I can't trust myself to BE myself until I know the other person isn't a flight risk."

When I spoke with her, Riddhi was debating what her next move should be with a guy she's been getting to know virtually during the COVID pandemic. "Dating right now, in quarantine times, all I ask for is consistent communication," she says. "I understand there are a lot of people working from home, but it is my belief that if you're trying to create a connection with me and we can't see each other, it shouldn't take eight to twelve hours to text me back. . . . I told my friend I plan on confronting that . . . but she feels I'm assigning an expectation to something that doesn't exist yet. I get her point, but . . . I personally don't see why I would even consider going forward if this need that is so important to me isn't met."

She's got a point: I don't see why Riddhi needs to pretend like she's cool with the texting thing, either. Trust me, I know suggesting she call him out so early on goes against one of the most sacred tenets of our beloved Game. But just indulge me for a second by playing out the four possible scenarios she's realistically looking at.

Option One: She Doesn't Call Him Out and Things Do Continue

Let's say Riddhi goes against her own nature and *doesn't* call this guy out. As far as he's concerned, nothing's wrong! So, things will likely keep going exactly as they are with him texting her every day or so and her growing more and more silently annoyed with him as he grows more and more interested in a version of her that's not really her at all. This option will likely lead her down the familiar path of bottling things up and ignoring red flags that she mentioned earlier.

The upside: Things are continuing.

The downside: She's unhappy and doesn't feel like she can fully be herself.

Option Two: She Doesn't Call Him Out and Things Don't Continue

What if Riddhi chooses to let it go and things still ultimately fizzle out between them? In other words, she bit her tongue and kept her annoyance to herself in an attempt to keep him around . . . only to lose him anyway.

The upside: None.

The downside: She just lost herself *and* her potential relationship.

Option Three: She Calls Him Out and He's *Not* Receptive to It

The fact of the matter is Riddhi very well might lose this guy if she goes ahead and calls him out for his bad texting habits. He could be put off or annoyed. Maybe he really is just an awful texter and needs to be with someone who can be chill about that. Unfortunately, that person isn't Riddhi. So, they end things.

The upside: She's now free to find someone who's capable of giving her what she wants.

The downside: She just lost a potential relationship with this guy.

Option Four: She Calls Him Out and He's Receptive to It

This is the best-case scenario. Riddhi takes the leap and shows her true colors and this guy is actually open to it. He embraces her blunt nature, and he makes the necessary changes. Even if he's not fully prepared to magically become a great texter, maybe they reach a compromise. Whatever the case, she's no longer annoyed and he's even more into her after having seen this glimpse of who she really is. In the future, Riddhi doesn't feel awkward bringing things up when she's bothered because she knows he can handle it, and in return, he feels more comfortable being himself because she was so totally herself with him.

The upside: She's just found a real connection with someone who truly appreciates her for who she is.

The downside: None. There's no downside in this scenario.

I don't know about you, but Options Three and Four seem like the best to me. Yes, Option Three leaves her without this guy. But, in that case, she can move on knowing he wasn't able to give her what she was looking for. To me, that far outweighs the possibility of keeping someone around even though their behavior makes your blood silently boil. Riddhi deserves to be with someone who appreciates her blunt nature. If that means weeding out the people who don't, then so be it.

I know what I'm suggesting here is scary. I mean, let's face it. The reason why so many of us continue to play The Game is because we've seen results. We dress up for a date and revel in the attention we get as a result. We refrain from blurting out, "I love you," at the end of the first date and it snags us a second date. We post thirst traps on Insta and, like clockwork, see their name pop up on our phones, seconds after. We keep playing The Game because, as far as we know, it *works*. It doesn't necessarily always help us "get the guy" (or girl or whoever you're into) in the long run, but it often helps us keep our crushes around for longer than expected.

And I'm not suggesting throwing The Game out entirely. Keep doing the things that feel true to your nature! If putting on a full face of makeup and doing your hair makes you feel like the most confident version of yourself before a first date, then go for it! Please! But if you feel like your best self with no makeup and a messy bun, then I don't see any issue with rocking that on your first date.

All I'm really suggesting here is that you stop playing The Game when it starts making you act like you have to be someone you're not. There's a fine line between playing The Game and losing yourself entirely—do yourself a favor and avoid crossing it.

Possibly my favorite story I heard when conducting interviews for this book came from 26-year-old Mayen of Bristol in the UK. "One of the biggest things I learnt from the last guy I dated before my current guy was never lie," she tells me via Instagram DM. Here's some backstory on that last guy, who was a friend of a friend living in her city when she first moved: "We met for dinner so he could, like, be my friend and like help me explore blah blah. But it quickly became flirty blah blah. Maybe the third time we hung out he was talking about girls and how they should be proper and all this and I just sat there holding a fart in like *oh boy this isn't going to work*." In other words, Mayen, who says she's been told by exes that she's "the gassiest gal they've ever met," tried to play The Game and all it left her with was a literal stomachache. Cut to her current boyfriend, the first person she dated after the non-farter. "When I met my boyfriend, I farted on our first date to make sure he knew me before I invested any real feelings." They've been together over two years now.

Now, I'm not suggesting you go ahead and loudly fart on your next first date. But I *am* suggesting you take some time to think about what your equivalent of a fart is. In other words, what aspect of yourself are you not willing to compromise on? What aspect of yourself do you want to make sure you're really getting out there immediately to ensure you're not wasting your time with someone who doesn't appreciate the *real* you? For example, my friend Tricia, a 29-year-old living in San Francisco, is one of the most confident people I know, and she tells me farting is pretty much the only thing she *is* willing to compromise on. "Other than holding back farts, I literally just don't think I know how to not be myself. Doesn't matter who the person is, I can't imagine being fake, let alone with a person you're actually trying to date," she says.

As you can probably imagine after that farting story, Mayen also has a radically authentic approach to dating. "In terms of 'playing the game,' I don't know how that can make meaningful connections," she says, using waiting to text back as an example. "I just never understood the wait to text because all you're doing is adding more anxiety on yourself. I think, being an anxious person, if I'm not honest I'm just anxious. So, I'd rather be honest and have someone be honest with me. From experience, the truth always comes out. And I don't know how many real relationships come from 'I waited three days to text him, then posted a pic of me and a guy friend on Instagram to make him jealous, and we've been happy ever since.'"

EUNICE	YOU
"Must hide all of my embarrassing quirks."	"Must show them all of my quirks ASAP so they know what they're getting into."

Mayen is right. Being authentic may be terrifying for a lot of us, but it's been scientifically proven to reap better rewards when it comes to finding relationships. A series of studies published in the journal *Personality and Individual Differences* in 2019[2] found authenticity to be a better dating strategy than game playing. To be clear, "game playing" was defined as hard-to-get behaviors (think: waiting to text back, acting aloof, et cetera) and "authenticity" was defined as both "taking risks for intimacy that might make you vulnerable to rejection" (think: sending the first text saying you had a nice time on your date) and "the unacceptability of deception, which requires honesty even if the truth might upset others" (think: Riddhi forcing herself to be honest and tell the guy she's not cool with his texting).

OK, I know I've already mentioned that this book isn't about figuring out how to "get" anyone, but if that *is* what you're trying to do . . . being yourself is the best way to do that. And you don't just have to take my word for it. I got to chat on the phone with Lawrence Josephs, PhD, the lead in the study, to talk about how, exactly, he was able to prove that being yourself is more successful than playing The Game. First, let's dive more deeply into how to be yourself. "Usually what being yourself meant was making yourself emotionally available, making yourself transparent, meeting the family, trusting casually—so basically just everyday behaviors that are like the antithesis of playing hard to get," Josephs explained to me on the phone. Some other ways to be yourself? Josephs suggests making yourself available to hang out with someone you want to hang out with, introducing them to your friends and family, and showing your emotional interest.

EUNICE	YOU
sitting on the couch with zero plans Gets text from crush: "Hey, you free to hang right now?" Responds: "Ah, no! So busy."	*sitting on the couch with zero plans* Gets text from crush: "Hey, you free to hang right now?" Responds: "Ya!"

So, what makes being yourself a better dating strategy than playing hard to get? For starters, being authentic makes you generally more attractive to others. For one of his studies, Josephs created two vignettes. In the first, the person is making themselves super accessible and approachable, while in the other, the person is playing hard to get and acting more stereotypically flirty. From there, he looked at which vignette was more attractive to participants and who found each vignette attractive. "Actually, everybody in general found the person who was being themselves more attractive," he tells me.

Next, there's the fact that being authentic will help you attract a better partner. "Do two birds of a feather flock together, or do opposites attract? Whenever they do research on it, it usually comes out that birds of a feather flock together," Josephs explains, adding that the "birds of a feather" principle is more scientifically called "assortative mating." In his research, Josephs tried to figure out if assortative mating extended itself to personality types. It turns out it does. "What I found is the more authentic you were, the more you were attracted to and wanted to date the authentic person in the vignette," he says. "And the more game-playing you were, the more you were attracted to the game-playing vignette."

So, yes! We've all had the experience where we played The Game and, to a degree, it has worked. But it most likely worked with someone who also *liked* to play games, which doesn't bode well for you guys in the future. "[If] two authentic people meet each other, they're going to be off to a great long-term relationship," Josephs explains. "If two game-playing people meet each other, and they're playing games with each other, they are probably going to have a very unstable relationship." I mean, does that really come as that much of a surprise? Think about your friend who *loves* "the chase." Who does she typically wind up with? Oh yeah, that's right. People who play hard to get.

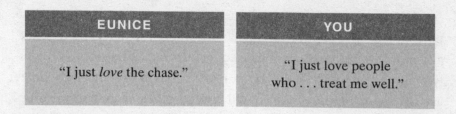

EUNICE	YOU
"I just *love* the chase."	"I just love people who . . . treat me well."

One last thing: Why do some people find it easier to be themselves than others? Well, I hope you were reading Step Four super carefully because it comes down to your relationship with rejection. "Authenticity is highly correlated with secure attachment," Josephs says. "So, basically, being yourself is more the dating strategy of resilience in people who can tolerate being themselves and getting rejected for it." In other words, if you feel like being yourself is a totally safe thing to do, you're going to be more open to letting your freak flag fly. "When people felt safe to be themselves, they were much quicker to return the text or set up a date," he explains. "When people were made to feel it was unsafe to be themselves, then they play hard to get. But, when you looked at it more deeply, this was more really like highly rejection-sensitive people were most likely to start playing hard to get when they didn't feel safe to be themselves."

In order to get over that incessant fear of rejection, Josephs recommends framing being yourself as a sort of screening strategy. "You might get rejected by a lot of more game-playing people before you find a more authentic person who reciprocates it, but then you're off and running," he says, adding you should look at the game-playing people who *do* reject you with more of a "good riddance" type attitude. "If that's your approach to dating, you're not wasting time with game-playing people," he says. "They might end up rejecting you for being authentic anyhow; then [it becomes] screening. You just have to have a hope that at some point you'll date somebody who is more authentic themselves and they'll appreciate you for who you are and then the relationship will click."

EUNICE	YOU
gets rejected	
"OMG, I just lost *The One*. How will I ever move on from this? I won't. I can't. I'll never find love with anyone ever again because I'm an unlovable loser."	*gets rejected* "Sayonara, loser."

If you're reading this and you're shaking your head because being yourself doesn't come naturally to you when dating, but you want an authentic relationship, don't sweat it too much. You can change! When I was doing research for this chapter, I posted a poll on my Instagram Stories asking people if they find it easy to be themselves when dating. "I just had this conversation with my best friend from high school," a 25-year-old in San Francisco—let's call her Kelsey—responded. "We were both saying earlier in life it was hard, but as we have grown up and know what we are looking for more, it's easier for us to be more ourselves while dating because we don't really want to waste our time. And it's also easier for us to identify when we aren't being ourselves in a dating situation because we know what that feels like!"

Kelsey wasn't the only person to answer with a story like that. Lots of women chimed in, saying that, with time, it became easier and easier for them to be themselves. I mean, even in my own experience, I know for a fact it was significantly easier for me to be myself while casually dating my current boyfriend than it was when I was casually dating Jack. The numbers in the YouGov survey supported this finding—when we asked women which game-playing behaviors they'd experienced in any of their past three relationships, women were less likely to have experienced any as they got older.[3] If you're more of a numbers person, here's how many women in each age bracket said they had not come across any of the (many) game-playing behaviors, from making partners jealous to waiting to respond to a text, in any of their past three relationships:

- 15 percent of women 18 to 34[4]
- 36 percent of women 35 to 54[5]
- 53 percent of women 55 and up[6]

So, yes. With time, you'll likely get over your reliance on The Game and, in turn, find it easier to just be yourself. But, in the meantime, if you don't really feel like you're totally there yet on your own, here are some dumb rules of The Game I'm begging you to just force yourself to be done with once and for all.

Pretending to Like What They Like

The Game: You're going to pretend to take interest in their interests— 9 percent of single women have done this, according to the YouGov survey, but that number jumped to 18 percent when adjusting for women between the ages of 18 and 34.[7]

IRL Example: Unnati, a 21-year-old from New York City, tells me she once memorized "all of Manchester United's player names and history" to prove to her crush she knew about the club, adding with a laugh that she still doesn't know much.

The Goal: The goal is to make them like you more by making them think you guys have *so* much in common.

Why It Needs to End: Because you *don't* actually have these things in common and you're effectively losing yourself in an attempt to make this person like you.

EUNICE	YOU
hears crush likes bird-watching	
has only watched the bird constantly pooping on her windowsill who she honestly kinda wishes would just die already	*hears crush likes bird-watching*
"OMG, I *love* bird-watching. Birds rule! Ha-ha, it's crazy. We have so much in common."	"Cool! I've never done that before."

Purposely Waiting Way Too Long to Text Back

The Game: They took twenty minutes to respond to your text, so you're going to take forty minutes to respond to theirs—according to the YouGov survey, 17 percent of single women have done this, with that number jumping to 28 percent for women between the ages of 18 and 34, and to 23 percent for women between the ages of 35 and 54.[8]

IRL Example: Penelope says she's always done this and, even with her current boyfriend, still catches herself doing this from time to time. "I recognize the absurdity of the rule of taking longer than a boy to text you back," she tells me, "but I still can't help but take a *bit* longer than I normally would, for fear of looking too eager or desperate."

The Goal: Make them think you're super busy and don't care too much about them.

Why It Needs to End: You're prolonging your own anxiety for . . . nothing. In no world is anyone going to think you're way cooler because you took forty minutes to text them back instead of twenty.

EUNICE	YOU
finally gets text from crush	
"I'll just sit here and stew for five to six more hours before responding because I'm a #coolgirl."	*finally gets text from crush*
	responds
spends rest of the day on the verge of throwing up with nerves	*spends rest of the day happily in conversation with crush*

Using Other People to Make Them Jealous

The Game: Purposely string other people along because you know it will bother the person you actually like—the YouGov survey found that 11 percent of single women ages 18 to 34 have done this.[9]

IRL Example: "I slept with the guy's best friend trying to make him jealous—oops," my friend Paige, a 25-year-old from Chicago, tells me. (A little backstory: Paige was on-again, off-again hooking up with her very good friend and coworker, a European guy who'd been living in the US, for about a year and a half. During one period when they were seeing other people, Paige wound up hooking up with his best friend, who was visiting from Europe.)

The Goal: To make the person you're into jealous, obvs.

Why It Needs to End: It rarely works the way you want it to and, more often than not, leaves everyone involved feeling bad. Take Paige, for example. After she slept with the best friend, she says, "he [her coworker] was very jealous." So, mission accomplished! But . . . she doesn't really feel great about the situation. "We are talking about [it], but it backfired since now I feel shitty for hurting him," she says.

EUNICE	YOU
talking to crush *only wants to be with crush* "Ha-ha, yeah, I actually am seeing so many people. My friends call me Kelis because there are *so* many boys in my yard."	*talking to crush* *only wants to be with crush* "I like you. And really only want to be with you."

Pretending You're Not Interested

The Game: You "play it cool" by pretending you're not that interested in a relationship—13 percent of women in the YouGov survey said that they avoided the DTR talk because they were afraid the relationship would fizzle if they admitted they had feelings, with that number jumping to 19 percent for women 18 to 34, then dropping to 11 percent for women 35 to 54, and 9 percent for women 55 and over.[10]

IRL Example: Tessa (from Step Four) not telling her college boy she had real feelings for him.

The Goal: Make them think you're cool (then fall in love with you).

Why It Needs to End: So many what-ifs are born from this dumb attempt at playing it cool. Eventually, an authentic person will just assume you're not interested and move on.

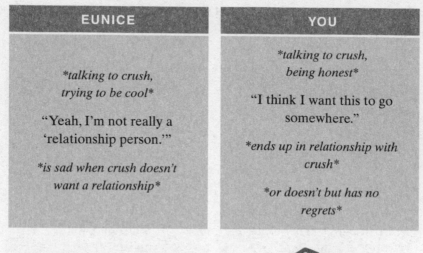

EUNICE	YOU
talking to crush, trying to be cool	*talking to crush, being honest*
"Yeah, I'm not really a 'relationship person.'"	"I think I want this to go somewhere."
is sad when crush doesn't want a relationship	*ends up in relationship with crush*
	or doesn't but has no regrets

Holding Back on Admitting Something Is Bothering You

The Game: Come off as "chill" by keeping any concerns to yourself—16 percent of single women in the YouGov survey reported they've not said if something was bothering them in the hopes that their partners would just understand without being told, with that number jumping to 21 percent for women between the ages of 18 and 34, holding steady at 17 percent for women between the ages of 35 and 54, and then dropping to 13 percent for women 55 and over.[11]

IRL Example: If Riddhi listens to her friend and lets the texting thing go.

The Goal: Make them like you more because they think you're so chill.

Why It Needs to End: Holding back on things that upset you is only going to make them bigger in your head and create a resentment toward the other person that isn't fair to either of you.

EUNICE	YOU
is annoyed with something crush did	
complains about it to everyone but her crush and slowly lets the small annoyance escalate in her mind to the point where it's all she can think about	*is annoyed with something crush did* *tells them and gets over it shortly after*

Like pretty much all of the Eunice-y things we do, the desire to submerge ourselves fully into the depths of The Game is, at its core, a result of our insecurity. Twenty percent of the women in the You-Gov survey[12] said they found trying to be themselves on a first date with someone they're into to be anxiety inducing, with that number jumping to 29 percent for women between the ages of 18 and 34. And it's partially that anxiety that makes The Game so appealing, right? Whether it's the first date or the fiftieth, whenever we're terrified of being ourselves, The Game gives us someone else to be. Then if we wind up getting rejected anyway it's no big deal because they didn't really reject *us*. They rejected the version of us we were presenting because The Game told us to. (Cue: Tessa's and my "Well, he never got to know the *real* me" rationale.)

But in exchange for that sense of comfort, we wind up relinquishing our own sense of self. Like I said before, casually playing The Game every now and then is no big deal. But things start getting dicey when we go in deep—when every move we make around our crushes is a calculated attempt at winning their affection.

"I am definitely known for being super obsessed very early on especially. I tend to really put all my focus and energy into a person I am interested in whether it be texting and making sure I've crafted the *best* response or even when I am talking to them, any content I send is very important and crucial as if it's the end of the world if the convo gets dry," my friend—let's call her Claire—a 25-year-old living in Boston, tells me. "So, I definitely feel like that's putting someone on too high of a pedestal especially since that stuff is *so* unimportant. But yes, every detail on how I present myself is very thoughtful [if] I really like the person . . . to avoid messing it up and 'losing the chance.' So dumb!!!"

In theory The Game, with all of its messages of letting them chase us and making ourselves busy, should serve as a reminder to put *ourselves* back on the pedestal. But, more often than not, all it winds up doing is placing our crushes on an even higher pedestal than we originally had them on. The more we commit to playing The Game, the more we magnify the other person's power over us. With each text we wait too long to respond to and with each lie we tell to make ourselves seem more appealing, we're subtly reaffirming this idea that we're not worthy of their affection exactly the way we are. So, of freaking course we're going to elevate them when we've created a narrative that says we're winners if we get their affection and we're losers if we don't. Because by playing The Game, we've effectively made them the prize. And if they're the prize where does that leave us?

Now, obviously, a happy relationship with someone you love from the bottom of your heart *is* a prize of sorts. But a truly happy relationship would be with the right person. And the right person does not need to be tricked into liking you.

Don't Be a Eunice . . .

- Just play The Game so long as it's making you feel *good*.
- Just stop playing The Game as soon as it starts spiking your anxiety.
- Just be as authentic as possible (and remember you're better off without the people who are turned off by that!).

The Big Send

After having gotten through the first six steps, it's time to . . . drumroll pleeeeease . . . *send it*. Remember, the "Text" in "Just Send the Text" is a metaphor. Your text can be anything—from finally making a move on your crush to blocking your ex on Instagram. Think of the text as your *truth*. It's the most "you" thing you can possibly think of doing with regard to your love life.

And however you choose to "Just Send the Text," it might come more easily to you now than it may have before reading this book. If you've followed along with the steps, at this point you've stopped playing games—from "Do They Like Me" to The Game. You've weeded out the toxic people in your life. You've stopped making excuses. You've gotten comfortable with rejection *and* with the idea of being single—even forever! You're by no means *trying* to be a chill girl to impress some guy (or girl or nonbinary person) but at this point you might be fairly, well . . . chill.

And yet there's one "Text" that still manages to shove even the most certified Chill Girl™ back down into Euniceville: the "What are we?" talk, or what I like to refer to as "The Big Send." *Dun dun dun*. On the off chance you're not familiar with it, the "what are we" talk is the oft-dreaded convo during which you go out on a limb and:

- Tell the person you have feelings for that you have feelings for them.
- Ask them if they see a future with you.

Does just the thought of having this conversation make you want to vomit all over this book? Well, you're not alone. It's so scary that only 13 percent of women in the YouGov survey[1] said they've initiated this conversation in any of their past three relationships. Moreover, 42 percent[2] said they've actively avoided the conversation for one reason or another.

But next time you're bugging about having this conversation, I'm here to help. There are two things you can do to take the pressure off of yourself before diving into The Big Send (but, really, they're helpful before you go for any type of send that feels a little scary).

DE-STRESSOR #1: DETHRONE THEM FROM THE PEDESTAL

Signs You've Got Them on a Pedestal

- ☐ Your characterization of them doesn't seem to match up to anyone else's.
- ☐ You're constantly trying to *make* them like you.
- ☐ You feel lucky to be receiving their attention.
- ☐ You can't think of a single thing wrong with them.
- ☐ You're quick to forget about or justify the straight-up-rude things they do to you.

Why You Put Them on a Pedestal: It's natural. We decide we're attracted to someone, and *boom*, we elevate them in our minds. And that's part of what makes that beginning infatuation phase so *fun*. This amazing person likes *us*. They want to give *us* attention. And the thrill of that can make for a fantastic high. But that's all it is. A high. And, like most highs, it also comes with some especially low lows that hit us hard when our phones *don't* light up with texts from them or they *don't* necessarily want to be exclusive with us.

IRL Example: Jenna, a 21-year-old living in Chicago, says she still struggles with placing her current boyfriend on a pedestal. "We have had very rocky on and off, but I often forget the things about him that make me really upset and the reason we broke up in the first place," she says, noting that he makes her feel "super insecure" and "less than" and that he can be "selfish." While things have admittedly improved with their tumultuous relationship, she still says she finds herself overlooking the cons. "Things have gotten better, but I for sure hype him up way more than he deserves, if that makes sense."

Why You Need to Take Them off the Pedestal: Why don't I do you one better and give you *three* reasons you need to take them off?

- Putting them on a pedestal creates an unbalanced power dynamic within the relationship that leaves you constantly trying to please them.
- As a result of the above, you have a harder time just being yourself around them.
- As a result of *both* of the above, the "relationship" you're building isn't grounded in any sort of reality— you don't really know them, and they don't really know you.

How to Dethrone Them: There are four antidotes here. First, like I said in the last chapter, stop playing games that have you bending over backward trying to "win" their affection.

The second thing you can do is give it time. *Really* get to know them. And let them *really* get to know you. This step is especially important before The Big Send. Before you go ahead and profess your feelings for someone, do yourself a favor and take the time to make sure those feelings are based on reality. Do they know the *real* you or do they know the perfectly curated version of yourself you've chosen to present them with? Do you see them as a real person or are they a flawless superhuman you're lucky to be getting attention from?

The third antidote is more for when you're in need of a quick fix. Let's say there's a "Text" you know you just *have* to send ASAP, but you're way too nervous. In this case, I'd recommend pulling out a piece of paper or the Notes app on your phone and making two side-by-side lists:

- **List One** outlines *at least* five flaws of this person. They can be as small as they pronounce the word "guarantee" weird or as big as they've lied to you on multiple occasions. The point is to humanize them. Everybody has faults.
- **List Two** outlines *at least* five great things about you. These are five reasons why anyone would be lucky to date you. If you can't think of any, ask your best friend or maybe one of your parents for help, but just make sure you get as many (or more!) things *right* with you as you have *wrong* with them in the other list.

Once you're done writing, look at the side-by-side lists and quickly remind yourself that the person you're interested in is just as lucky to be with you as you've convinced yourself you are to be with them.

A Glimpse into Your New Pedestal-Free Life: When Lola, a 23-year-old from Knoxville, Tennessee, stopped putting people on the pedestal, she wound up meeting her now fiancé. "I used to keep all of my significant others on a pedestal that literally I couldn't even reach, and they failed me every single time," she tells me via Instagram DM. "When I finally put myself on the pedestal instead of some asshole, I actually met my now fiancé. When you are a natural giver it's hard not to do that, but when you figure out your worth . . . it's easy to decide who belongs on there and who doesn't!"

Now, I'm not saying the minute you stop putting people on the pedestal, you're going to find your soul mate like Lola did. But you *will* be setting yourself up to have more stress-free, authentic connections. Without the pedestal, you're free to be part of a connection that involves two people seeing each other for who they really are—flaws and all—and still (excitedly!) choosing to be with each other. Yes, you still may get that high feeling when their name pops up on your phone. But this time the high is grounded in reality.

EUNICE	YOU
"I'm so lucky to be with someone so *perfect*! Gah, I hope I don't mess this up."	"I'm so happy I finally found someone worthy of me. I can't wait to get to know them more."

DE-STRESSOR #2: LAY OFF YOUR SQUAD-TURNED-ADVISORS*

Signs You're Too Reliant on Your Squad-Turned-Advisors

☐ You break down every interaction you have with your crush with multiple friends.

☐ You can't respond to any of your crush's texts without running it by your friends.

☐ You often feel torn on which friend's advice to take regarding your love life.

☐ You second-guess your own instincts because your friends would handle your situation differently.

☐ You feel like you need the relationship to progress at a certain pace because that's what your friends expect.

Why You Keep Your Squad-Turned-Advisors on Staff: There are so many reasons why we rely on our friends and family heavily with regard to our love lives, but the main one is we're confused. We're confused about whether or not our crushes like us. We're confused about how to *keep* them liking us. We're confused about what to reply to their texts. And, most important for a lot of us, we're confused about when and how to take whatever this is to the next level. It's only natural for us to want to turn to our trusted inner circle (and maybe a friendly Trader Joe's clerk or two) for advice when we feel so totally lost.

---

* And by "your squad-turned-advisors," I'm obviously referring to the squad of friends/coworkers/family members/strangers all of us have helping us calculate our every move with regard to our crushes.

IRL Example: "Their opinion definitely matters," a 24-year-old woman splitting her time between Beirut and New York—let's call her Allie—tells me via Instagram. "I'm from a small city with very small social circles, so whenever I date a local, my friends always know them way better than I do, so that plays a huge role. I also am the type that wants my friends to call me out on my bullshit if I'm being unreasonable. But it always ends up being a situation where I ask too many people for their opinion and my own feelings get validated and invalidated by so many people at the same time that they kind of get lost and I forget how *I* personally feel about situations." She adds that her reliance on her friends "stems a bit from me being very insecure around men and so I always think other people know better."

Why You Need to Lay Them Off: Relying on our friends for advice on every little thing is a sneaky stressor because it's something we *think* will reduce our stress. We get panicked about what to reply to our crush's text or how to go about initiating The Big Send, so we turn to our friends for help. But all that really happens is we wind up turning up the volume on what everyone else thinks we're supposed to be doing with regard to our love lives and, in doing so, turning *down* the volume on our own instincts. When this process starts happening, three stressful things take place:

- **We're left second-guessing ourselves:** Let's say you get a "hey, how ya doing?" text from your crush. You screenshot the text and immediately send it in a group text to your best friend and your sister. Your sister immediately responds: "OMG text them back right now inviting them to be your date to my engagement party." You love the idea, and you trust your sister's opinion. (I mean, after all, the woman is getting *married*. She has to know what she's doing.) You're sold. You send the text and as you're happily browsing Rent the Runway dresses your best friend chimes in: "Sorry, guys. I was in a meeting, but OMG, Eunice, NO. Do not do that. It is WAY too soon." Your stomach drops. You immediately exit out of Rent the Runway and divert to figuring out how to unsend the text message you were so excited about just twenty seconds ago.

- **The people we date don't get to know the *real* us:** Let's keep that same example going for a second here. No matter whose advice you choose to take, neither was really what *you* wanted, right? Inviting them to the wedding is what your sister would have done. Playing it cool is what your best friend would have done. But the bottom line is this person (I hope) isn't interested in your best friend or your sister. No, they're interested in *you*.

- **We dull down our own instincts:** The biggest risk of asking your best friend and your sister—or whoever you have on your advisory squad—about what they would do with regard to your love life is it moves you further away from your own intuition. Every time you ask your friends and family what they would do, rather than taking the time to really think about what *you* would do, you're subtly telling yourself your own instincts aren't good enough. Your instincts are a muscle just like any other. If you don't use them, they'll weaken.

When done in excess, all asking your loved ones for advice really ever winds up doing is making things so much more complicated than necessary. Your sister may tell you to go for it, and your best friend may tell you it's *way* too soon and you absolutely cannot. Then what? You're left confused, stuck, and stressed, as you have to choose between disappointing your best friend or your sister. Not to mention the fact that, in the process, you've completely lost sight of what it is *you* want to do.

How to Lay Them Off: Nobody is saying you have to shut your friends out of your love life entirely. I mean, if you think keeping all the details of your romantic life to yourself would make you feel less stressed, then please, by all means, go for it. But, if you're like me, and you feel like you're lying if you don't divulge every detail to your best friends, then just try going with a little flip of the script.

Right now, the stress-inducing system you likely have in place goes a little something like this:

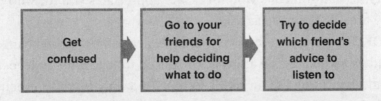

Instead, try revamping it to something like this:

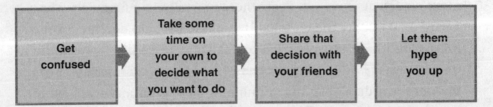

In other words, decide what you want to do, then *tell them* you're doing it. Especially with The Big Send, it's so important that it's something *you* genuinely want to do. Have the conversation because you feel like it's the right time and say whatever it is *you* want to say. Your friends can be there on the sidelines to hype you up and help you. But that's where they should stay for this.

Even if you're not clear on exactly what you should do, come to a—singular!—friend with a few options *you* have come up with on your own. Make it clear you want to go with one of these options and have them help you weigh out the pros and cons of each. Oh, and! If that one friend is strongly urging you to go with one of your options and your gut is screaming at you that you should go with another, then forget the friend and go with your gut.

A Glimpse into Your Life Advice-Free: Imagine a world where you trust your own instincts with ease. A world where you're able to just accept that this person is falling for you—not your friend, your co-worker, your family member, or a nice stranger you met at the grocery store. *You.* You give people you like the chance to get to know the real you, and in turn, you give yourself a chance to find something authentic with someone who loves and appreciates you for who you really are. It's as simple as that.

OK, in reality, your life may not be *that* easy-breezy. But laying off the advisory board is an approach I started to take after college and it made my dating life infinitely better—not only because it helped me find my current relationship, one where I have a boyfriend who truly appreciates me for who I really am, but because it made me feel more confident in myself. Yeah, there are still some moments when I panic and ask my friends what they think I should do. But, for the most part, I have actively tried to challenge myself to figure it out on my own, *then* turn to my friends. It made my relationships, even the ones that didn't pan out, a million times better and—way more important—made me feel more confident.

EUNICE	YOU
"My friends told me I need to define this relationship, so I'm defining this relationship even though in my gut I feel like it's way too soon and I'm not ready."	"I'm going to define this relationship because I feel like now is the perfect time to do that."

Now that we've all de-stressed, let's get down to the nitty-gritty of The Big Send. Honestly, I could write a whole separate book solely devoted to this conversation. I have lots of thoughts on the matter and have spent lots (and lots!) of time researching everything about it, from individual experiences with it to psychologists' takes on how it should be executed.

Actually, if you want some hand-holding with regard to every little detail of The Big Send, I'd highly recommend reading an article I wrote for Tinder Swipe Life in November 2019 called "Your Complete Guide to the DTR Talk."[3] The title is accurate. It will walk you through every single little step in extreme detail.

But, because so much of Sending the Text has to do with trusting your own instincts, I'm going to keep my advice *here* simple with just three relatively broad mini steps.

MINI STEP ONE: PICK THE RIGHT TIME

And no. I don't mean pick the right time for them or for your friends or for what feels socially acceptable. I mean pick the right time for *you*.

For some people, that time might be never. And there are some signs avoiding this conversation altogether might be the best course of action for you:

☐   You want to keep things casual—8 percent of women in the YouGov survey[4] said they held off on having the "What are we?" talk because they wanted to keep things casual.

☐   You aren't sure if you wanted to stay in the relationship—14 percent of women[5] in the YouGov survey said this is why they avoided the conversation.

☐   You're naturally a game-playing person who would prefer to drop hints and hopefully have the person you're into pick up what you're putting down.*

---

* But just remember Josephs's research! That tactic is probably going to leave you playing games on loop with someone who also enjoys playing them.

Or maybe it's not that you *never* want to go for The Big Send but just that you're not ready *yet*. Here are some signs the time hasn't quite come yet:

☐ You're still trying to figure out what you want with them—9 percent of women[6] in the YouGov survey said this is why they held off on the "What are we?" talk.

☐ You still have them up on a too-high pedestal.

☐ You still don't think you could execute The Big Send without your friends telling you *exactly* what to say.

☐ You have external circumstances that are, quite frankly, making you too stressed to deal with The Big Send currently.

Let me elaborate a bit on that last one real quick. Usually I'm Team Go for The Big Send as soon as you feel like you're ready to take things to the next level. Also, as you know based on all my ramblings in Step Four, I'm not one for letting your fear of rejection stop you from really putting yourself out there. *But* the fact of the matter is life isn't always "normal." Sometimes there are curveballs—whether it be a pandemic, a war, or even just a really bad day—that might make you more inclined to keep things the way they are because you just don't feel like dealing with the stress of changing the status quo.

For example, a 28-year-old woman—let's call her Marie—tells me over Instagram DM that she's been hooking up with a guy she knew from high school while they're both quarantining in their childhood homes during COVID-19. The thing is, they also happen to both live in the same city during normal non-pandemic life. "We've been 'dating' for a month now and really like each other," she says. "We say that but haven't talked as much about what happens when we go back to [the city we both regularly live in]. We've both been pretty clear we aren't just in this to hook up, but both of us are still not taking the convo anywhere towards next steps." She adds: "I think a reason for me not bringing it up is being afraid of rejection but also knowing the conversation is gonna change what we have right now which is really nice."

If you've got something bringing you joy in an otherwise unjoyful time and you're worried that going for The Big Send might bring about a change you're not ready to deal with, then I say keep doing what makes you feel good. It's time for The Big Send when, unlike Marie, you *are* ready to change what you have right now. You're ready to take that plunge when keeping things at the status quo is no longer cutting it and when the anxiety of keeping things as is outweighs the sadness of potentially losing them altogether.

If there's no external crisis going on and you *are* sure that you're ready for something more with this person, it's probs time to consider having this conversation. You'll know it's time for The Big Send when you:

☐ Have spent a sufficient amount of time together—according to Match's 2019 "Singles in America" survey, the average single person wants to wait four months[7] before having this talk, but the point isn't to just spend however many months together. The point is to take the time to *really* get to know them and, in turn, let them get to know you. (Spoiler: If you think they're perfect, it's not time yet.)

☐ Have decided you *want* to take things to the next level—not just because you feel like you should!

☐ Have come to the conclusion this is someone who enhances your life—not a time-wasting tampon.

☐ Know things are no longer cutting it for you exactly as they are.

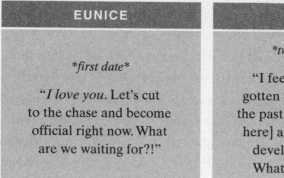

EUNICE	YOU
first date "*I love you.* Let's cut to the chase and become official right now. What are we waiting for?!"	*twentieth date* "I feel like I've really gotten to know you over the past [insert time frame here] and I'm starting to develop real feelings. What do you think?"

Decided it's time for The Big Send? OK, great, let's move on to Mini Step Two.

MINI STEP TWO: SEND IT

I know The Big Send can be terrifying. Even if you're the most confident person in the world, making yourself vulnerable adds an element of fear. And, oftentimes, the fear that comes along with it can be so big that you avoid the conversation altogether. Here are the most common reasons why people don't go for The Big Send, based on the YouGov survey:

- It felt awkward (16 percent avoided because of this).[8]
- They were afraid of getting rejected (15 percent avoided because of this).[9]
- They were afraid things would fizzle out if they said something (13 percent avoided because of this).[10]

And all of those reasons are legitimate! It *might* be awkward. You *might* get rejected. Things *might* fizzle out. But let's explore the alternative here for a second. Let's imagine that you don't say anything because you're too scared of any or all of the above and just keep things status quo, even though you're not happy with things the way they are. Now you're stuck in the familiar emotional prison that is relationship purgatory—as I mentioned in the first step, 18 percent of women in the YouGov survey said they've been in a relationship purgatory where the relationship never got defined.[11]

If this has never happened to you, let me paint you a picture of what being stuck pretending you're OK with keeping things "casual" often looks like: Countless rounds of the "Do They Like Me" Game, lots of drunk cries, losing yourself entirely as you try to master The Game, and, finally, an inevitable fizzle that leaves you with a million what-ifs.

So, no. I don't recommend relationship purgatory. If you're ready to take the relationship to the next level, do yourself a favor and *say something*. I promise the anxiety that comes along with maintaining things as they are will far outweigh the anxiety that comes along with losing them altogether.

As for *what* you actually say, I'll leave that up to you. The only rule of Just Sending the Text, whether it be a response to your crush's casual text or The Big Send, is the "Text" has to be *yours*. It has to be totally and completely true to *you*. So, I'm not going to tell you exactly what to say or how to say it. And I hope you don't turn to anyone else for a script, either. Remember what you're essentially asking for is a relationship, and if you do enter a relationship with this person, this will be the first of *many* difficult/awkward/weird/vulnerable conversations.

If you really are feeling lost in the what-to-say department, just try to, in your own way, hit these two points:

- Be honest about how you feel about them.
- Be clear on what you're asking of them: A relationship with "labels"? Being exclusive with no labels? Some clarity on where this is going? Emmalee Bierly, LMFT and one of the hosts of the *ShrinkChicks* podcast, highlighted the importance of doing this in that Tinder article I mentioned earlier, and I'd be doing you a

disservice if I didn't include it here. "Just because I say that we're dating doesn't mean that you automatically know I mean we're not sleeping with anyone else," Bierly said in the article. "Do not assume. Define what a relationship looks like for you, because we don't all have the same idea."[12]

And don't stress too much if you mess it up! Maybe you get interrupted halfway through. Maybe you get too nervous and just start rambling about something totally unrelated and have to try again a few times before actually mustering up the courage to say something. Just go at your own pace and forgive yourself if you don't get it *exactly* right.

EUNICE	YOU
"You know what? This conversation is just too scary. I'm going to avoid it altogether."	"I'm not looking *forward* to this conversation. But I'm no longer happy with things the way they are, so I need to have it to set myself free from relationship purgatory."

MINI STEP THREE: STICK TO IT

And this one is *key*. If the person you want to be with does not want the same thing as you or does not feel the same way about you, walk away. For your own sanity and your own self-worth, please just put one foot in front of the other and walk away. Take Bailey, for example. Bailey is a 25-year-old living in Atlanta, Georgia, and she tells me she's gotten to the point where she's "sick" of not defining her relationships because she's no longer down for keeping things casual. "So, after seeing this guy for three months, I had brought up my intentions a few times. Finally, because it felt like a true relationship (based on the way we were acting, the deeper conversations/topics we were getting into, and sharing the things we were going through in our lives), I told him I wanted to make things official and he agreed," she recalls. "No more than three weeks go by when he decides he really just wanted to keep things exactly the way they were, but without the title. He then wanted to continue to see me/talk to me the same amount and in the same way, but didn't want me to think we would be moving this towards a relationship, because he just 'wasn't ready for that' . . . so I said 'See ya.' It's just frustrating that guys want the same privileges of a boyfriend without being your boyfriend."

I know exactly what Bailey means because I've been there. When I was seeing my "He's Perfect, But" guy, I eventually got to a point—about four months in—where I realized just having these 24/7 conversations and sporadically flying to see each other wasn't enough. I didn't necessarily need us to be in a relationship at that very moment; I just needed to know this was eventually going somewhere. So, I mustered up all my courage and asked him if he thought it was. He essentially said no and that he didn't understand why we couldn't just keep things exactly like they were. I eventually caved and said I'd be cool with just maintaining the status quo. Obviously, I did this with the hope that maybe he would eventually change his mind or that he'd move to New York and things would magically work out. And I'm not the only one who's done this—as I mentioned earlier, 17 percent of women in the YouGov survey[13] said they've compromised the relationship they're having with the hope that their partner's feelings would change over time.

But all I did by making that compromise was make myself more miserable. I thought I was sparing myself the pain of actually having to cut ties with him, but instead I just created a new pain, as I was actively trying to be with someone who made it exceedingly clear that he didn't like me as much as I liked him. And let me tell you, that dynamic doesn't exactly do wonders for the ol' self-esteem. Eventually things fizzled out between us, but because I'd let things go on for so long it was ten times messier than it needed to be. He felt hurt that I was pulling away after telling him I was fine keeping things the way they were, and I felt equal parts guilty for hurting him and mad at myself for not telling him I *wasn't* fine when I originally had the chance to.

Even on the off chance this person *does* eventually cave and want a relationship with you, things might not shape up to be the happily ever after you were hoping for. "This guy I was dating and I were having the 'where is this going convo' and I assume I said I wanted it to continue and wanted more and wanted to date (I don't really remember what I said but that's what I wanted) and he came back with some 'qualms' he had and listed them and I was like 'okkkaaayyy' and we kinda just kept seeing each other," my friend— let's call her Malia, a 25-year-old living in San Francisco—tells me via Instagram DM. "Probs a month or so later he ended up asking me to be his GF. A few months later he broke things off. Looking back, I really should've paid attention to those qualms 'cause really those were the first flags that he didn't really deep down want to be with me."

We all deserve to be with people who aren't just casually down to date us. We deserve to be with people who enthusiastically (!!!!) want to date us. People who are excited by the idea that we like them, not scared or turned off by it. If someone tells you they have hesitations or they don't feel the same way as you, believe them and move on. Don't waste your time trying to convince someone you're worthy of theirs.

EUNICE	YOU
gets rejected	
"OK, well, maybe we can just keep hanging out for a few months or years until maybe you decide to like me back!?"	*gets rejected* "Your loss, *bye*."

Don't Be a Eunice . . .

- Just go for The Big Send when you're ready to.
- Just move on if they don't want the same thing as you do.
- Just take the time to de-stress before sending any "Text."

Keeping
the Faith

That's *it*. This book is essentially an extremely long-winded, seven-step reminder to be yourself. Because that's all Just Sending the Text really boils down to, right? Be yourself. And, more important, value yourself. Put yourself first. Prioritize your own needs. If something isn't serving you, then stop doing that thing. Even if that thing is what everyone tells you that you need to do in order to find your very own happily ever after.

But what if you read all seven steps and still don't feel like you've mastered this whole Just Send the Text thing? What if you still find yourself feeling like a Eunice every time even the very thought of your crush pops into your mind? The secret to Just Sending the Text, and most other things in life, is that there's no such thing as "mastering" it. At the end of the day, most of us will still be Eunices every now and then because, well, we're human. Reading one book isn't just going to magically erase years of learned anxiety.

Even when I met my current boyfriend, Brian, and things were going pretty much as smooth as humanly possible, I'd find the Eunice part of my brain occasionally screaming things like, *SOS: He still has the Bumble app on his phone!! No, you guys aren't exclusive. But still! This is bad! Swallow it! Don't say anything! Chill Girls never say anything!*

The only difference between my experience with Brian and my experience when I was seeing Jack is that I no longer let the Eunice part of my brain control me. Rather than letting myself silently sink into panic mode when I saw that he had Bumble on his phone, I brought it up. It took two tries (and I threw up the first time*), but, finally, I said it. And you know what? It wasn't a big deal. He deleted it from his phone right there, and we became exclusive that day. But, looking back, it's what I *personally* got out of it that really matters: I proved to myself that I can have a difficult conversation, even if it meant sacrificing my "cool" factor. And, in having that conversation, I proved to myself that I'm worthy of a certain level of respect. If something makes me uncomfortable, I don't *have* to silently suffer. I'm allowed to say something. I'm allowed to end the suffering.

Mastering Just Sending the Text is really just respecting yourself. And you're doing so by always choosing to do the thing that feels true to you, even if that's the scarier option in the moment. I say "always" because you're going to have to make this decision over and over and over again. There are going to be a million and one moments during which your old Eunice-y thoughts will start creeping back into your head and you're going to have to actively remind yourself to Just Send the Text. Because that's what you deserve. That's what you owe to yourself.

---

* Nope, not kidding. Was so nervous that I legitimately puked.

Fifty Times to Remind Yourself to Just Send the Text

1. When you're trying to decide what their "hii" text really means.
2. When you're about to play any round of the "Do They Like Me" Game.
3. When you go to put on the uncomfortable heels you hate because you're worried it's weird to wear sneakers on a first date.
4. When you're dying to tell them about your super obscure passion but are worried it will turn them off.
5. When you want to go for The Big Send but are too scared of how awkward it will make things.
6. When you want to go for The Big Send but are too scared of getting rejected.
7. When you don't want to go for The Big Send but are feeling pressured to by your friends.
8. When you realize you can't name one thing wrong with them.
9. When you're dating a human tampon.
10. When you're staring at the clock waiting for it to be an appropriate time for you to respond to your crush.
11. When you're holding off on sending the first text, even though you're absolutely dying to, just because you feel like they should be chasing you.
12. When you're going through every possible way this could end in flames in your head.
13. When your great-aunt is making you feel awful for being single.
14. When you're comparing yourself to all of your friends in relationships.
15. When you're about to settle because you think it's better than being single.

16. When they don't watch your Instagram Story.

17. When they do watch your Instagram Story.

18. When you thought you were ready for a relationship, but a pandemic hits and you're actually not quite ready to handle that sort of conversation.

19. When you have the urge to swallow your own feelings down because you want to be "cool."

20. When you want to blame the hookup culture for how single you are.

21. When you want to blame dating apps for how single you are.

22. When you want to blame social media for how single you are.

23. When you're about to post a screenshot of your most recent text thread to your GroupMe.

24. When you're given the choice between a downward spiral and an upward spiral.

25. When you're about to type your crush's ex's name into your Instagram search bar.

26. When you feel upset that you ended things but like you have to pretend like it's fine because it wasn't a "real" relationship.

27. When you're up at four in the morning stressing about your love life.

28. When you're trapped in relationship purgatory.

29. When you see someone you're super attracted to from across the room.

30. When you're about to commit to trapping yourself in relationship purgatory.

31. When someone tries to tell you happily ever after has to involve a romantic partner.

32. When you're tempted to blame the hookup culture for everything that's wrong with your love life.

33. When you're tempted to blame dating apps for everything that's wrong with your love life.

34. When you're tempted to blame social media for everything that's wrong with your love life.

35. When seeing their pictures on your Instagram feed makes you so anxious you could puke.

36. When you have the urge to see what would have happened if you just shot your shot with that crush from high school.

37. When you're feeling sad because all your friends are in relationships, but you're still single.

38. When you're going on hour two of fine-tuning the "Hey! What are you up to?" text you're about to send your crush.

39. When you're calling the third friend to consult on exactly what your next move should be with your crush.

40. When you're supposed to be working but are, instead, focusing all your energy on trying to figure out how they really feel about you.

41. When you want to block them but are secretly scared of shutting down the chance of them coming back to you.

42. When you're playing games that aren't making you feel good.

43. When you start feeling like winning their attention is like winning the lottery.

44. When you're too embarrassed to be sad about ending things with your hookup buddy because you "weren't even official."

45. When you're making yourself more anxious by trying to be "chill."

46. When you feel like you have to be someone you're not to get this person to like you.

47. When you feel like having a significant other is an indication of your self-worth.

48. When you're being driven crazy by the person you like.

49. When your friends gave you contradictory pieces of advice and now you're totally confused.

50. Whenever you feel like just being yourself is no longer good enough.

That's what my relationship has been. Four years of the two of us actively choosing to be vulnerable, to be ourselves, to do the "uncool" thing and put ourselves out there . . . all the while being reassured by the other person that someone loves us for exactly who we are.

I've been really hesitant about using my current relationship as an example for anything throughout this book because the goal has never been to use the Just Send the Text method to score us relationships. I'd hate for you to read this entire thing and come out of it thinking, *OK, this is a new way for me to con someone into falling for me! It worked for Candice, so it should work for me!* No, that's not the point.

Even before I met Brian, Just Sending the Text helped me overcome a lot of my dating anxiety. It made me happier, it made me more comfortable in my own skin, and it made me more *myself.* Those things are what make this method special. Those aspects of it are what "worked" for me.

Brian and I could break up tomorrow and I'd be sad—so sad!— but I'm confident I'd still be able to stand strong on my own two feet. I wouldn't feel like less of a person because he didn't want to be with me. And there's not one thing I would regret looking back on our relationship. I wouldn't feel like I left anything unsaid or left any enjoyable moment together not enjoyed to the absolute fullest. So, if he chose to dump me tomorrow, I'd ultimately have to say good riddance because, well, he knew me. He knew all of me. And if that wasn't for him, then he wasn't for me. I'm better off on my own than I am trying to alter myself for someone who doesn't accept me completely as I am.

This book isn't about "getting the guy" (or the girl, or the nonbinary person) and I hope I've already made that clear. But if "getting" someone is what you're after, don't you want what you find with them to be *real*?

True love, the kind we all deserve to find, isn't born from stress and anxiety and pretending. It's born from joy. It's calm. It's warm. It's *authentic.*

If that's the sort of love you're after, then do yourself a favor and Just Send the Text.

ACKNOWLEDGMENTS

Everyone Who Contributed: Specifically, the fifty-five people who shared their sometimes extremely personal stories and opinions with me for the making of this book. This was by no means a solo endeavor. I mean, can you imagine if the entire book was just me rambling on about my own life for hundreds of pages? You guys made this book. So, thank you.

Dad: I feel silly writing you a small paragraph in this little dinky section when truly outlining what makes you the only real Best Dad Ever would require its own anthology. I'll try to dilute it all down to this: Thank you for raising me to be the best me that I could possibly be. This book wouldn't have existed if I didn't have a dad who raised me to be nuts enough to think that I could do whatever I set my mind to. You gave me the courage to do things outside the norm and to dream outside the box. I love you so much and I hope that when I have children I can be maybe just a fraction as good of a parent to them as you've been to me.

Mom: You already got multiple pages in the book, so I'll keep it short. I love you. Thank you for making me feel endlessly loved and for very much inspiring this book.

Brian: On our first date when I told you what I did for a living you gave me a high five and said that was awesome. I don't necessarily believe in the idea of just "knowing," especially not on the first date, but I definitely had a strong feeling that we'd work at that point. I could never even possibly imagine being with someone more supportive of me and of everything I do than you.

Nilou: Thank you for being the first person I trusted to read this entire book and the first person I've trusted with pretty much everything my whole life. Thank you for letting me co-opt your life for content. Thank you for just always being there for everything I've ever needed no matter what (even when I'm annoying you).

Book Advisory Board: Nobody outside the publishing industry should have to read and revise as many sentences as you guys had to read and revise. Momo, you, along with my mom, helped inspire this book's message. Spongey, there would be no toilet metaphor if it weren't for you. Anne, our brainstorm sessions are the reasons why half the topics in this book are even covered. If this book is a best seller, I owe you all a vacation (or a fast-casual dinner; IDK how much money a best seller would actually make me, lol).

Kevin and Alexia: Oh man, where to even begin!? You guys championed this book before it was even a book! From reading multiple drafts of the proposal, to contributing to the actual book, to helping me brainstorm my way out of multiple bouts of writer's block, this book would absolutely not be here if it were not for you two.

Nora: You pretty much gave me free rein over your life's stories for this, and I can't thank you enough. I love you sooo much; thanks for helping make this book what it is and thanks for just being a great friend when I was frazzled trying to finish this.

Alina: I know those transcriptions were probably so incredibly boring for you, but there is truly no way I would have been able to finish this book in time if it wasn't for your help. Like, did you read Step Six?! The bulk of it wouldn't have existed without your help. Thank you *so* much.

Cori: Thank you for going above and beyond when it came to sharing your personal experiences for this book. Also thank you for spending so much time talking through so many of my ideas with me. I love you so much and I cannot *wait* for your wisdom to make its way over to people who aren't lucky enough to call you one of their best friends.

The Paradise Sisters: Abby and Alex, you *both* helped me make this book into a thing before I even had a book deal. Alex, you coming over and sharing your stories with me that night just to help me have enough intel to put my proposal together truly meant the world. Abby, you recruited friends to share stories that truly made this book so much better and gave me such great intel as to what people your age are stressing about in terms of dating. *Thank you.*

Amy: I chose you as my agent because you didn't just believe in *me*; you believed in this book. I could tell from the moment you emailed me that you Got It. You truly understood what I was trying to say with this, and you made sure my message was never compromised. Thank you for believing in this message as fiercely as I do.

Ronnie: You made this book better. Like, so much better. When I reread the entire book and realized the only chapter that I had to redo was the first chapter it was no coincidence considering the first chapter is the only one I created before I had your input. I could not have handpicked a better editor for my first book. You respected my voice the whole way through, you adhered to my extremely type A writing schedule, and you helped refine this book to the absolute best possible version. Thank you.

The YouGov Team: Thank you for honoring an agreement that was made before many of you were even on board. The data you provided set this book over the edge and made it feel like it was bigger than just a rambling of my own opinions. I'm so excited to get the data you collected out into the world.

Kate: Thank you so much for helping me make the survey that set this book over the edge! Moreover, thank you for providing me with insights that made this book something people could truly relate to.

Laura and Lauren: I could have written the greatest, most helpful book in the world, and without great marketing and publicity, the fact is it wouldn't matter. Thank you for helping make sure my book had its fair shot at getting out into the world.

Patrick: My book has a cover and is filled with artwork that I love. Thank you so much for bringing it to life in such a beautiful way.

Lewelin: You took a string of words in a Word document and transformed them into a beautiful, well-polished *book*. Thank you for making me feel like a legitimate author.

Theresa: Without your faith this book would have never come to fruition the way that it has. Thank you for allowing me to join the Tiller family. I couldn't have chosen a better home for my first book!

Barbara: THANK YOU for making sure my book looks polished and professional. Your help made me feel like a real Author (capital "A" intended!).

Laura and Annie: Thank you so much for making sure everything was produced in a timely manner—no easy feat in the midst of a global pandemic. Timeliness was everything for this book and I truly can't thank you both enough.

NOTES

STEP ONE: TAKING CONTROL OF YOUR INNER EUNICE

1. YouGov on behalf of Candice Jalili, *Relationship Book*, March 13, 2020, distributed by YouGov.
2. YouGov, *Relationship Book*.
3. YouGov, *Relationship Book*.
4. YouGov, *Relationship Book*.
5. YouGov, *Relationship Book*.
6. YouGov, *Relationship Book*.
7. YouGov, *Relationship Book*.
8. YouGov, *Relationship Book*.
9. YouGov, *Relationship Book*.
10. "Singles in America," Match, 2019, https://www.singlesinamerica .com/.
11. YouGov, *Relationship Book*.
12. YouGov, *Relationship Book*.
13. Candice Jalili, "Dating + Social Media: The New Rules," *Cosmopolitan*, May 2018, 109–13.
14. Candice Jalili, "DUI: Dating Under the Influence," *Cosmopolitan*, January 2018.
15. Candice Jalili, "7 Dating Pressures You Can Just Go Ahead and Ignore," Swipe Life, Tinder, July 24, 2019, https://swipelife.tinder.com /post/dating-stress.
16. YouGov, *Relationship Book*.
17. "Singles in America," Match, 2019, https://www.singlesinamerica .com/.

18. "Singles in America," Match, 2019, https://www.singlesinamerica.com/.

19. Michael J. Rosenfeld, Reuben J. Thomas, and Sonia Hausen, "Disintermediating Your Friends: How Online Dating in the United States Displaces Other Ways of Meeting," *Proceedings of the National Academy of Sciences* 116, no. 36 (September 3, 2019): 17753–58, https://doi.org/10.1073/pnas.1908630116.

20. YouGov, *Relationship Book.*

21. YouGov, *Relationship Book.*

STEP TWO: REWRITING HAPPILY EVER AFTER

1. YouGov, *Relationship Book.*

2. YouGov, *Relationship Book.*

3. Rae Alexandra, "Is 'The Bachelor' Franchise's Popularity Rooted in Fear of Social Progress?," KQED, August 9, 2018, https://www.kqed.org/pop/104953/is-the-bachelor-franchises-popularity-rooted-in-fear-of-social-progress.

4. Wendy Wang and Kim Parker, "Record Share of Americans Have Never Married," Pew Research Center's Social & Demographic Trends Project, Pew Research Center, September 24, 2014, https://www.pewsocialtrends.org/2014/09/24/record-share-of-americans-have-never-married.

5. "All the Single Ladies: 61% of Women in the UK Are Happy to Be Single Compared to 49% of Men," Mintel, November 13, 2017, https://www.mintel.com/press-centre/social-and-lifestyle/all-the-single-ladies-61-of-women-in-the-uk-are-happy-to-be-single-compared-to-49-of-men.

6. Stephanie S. Spielmann, Geoff MacDonald, Jessica A. Maxwell, Samantha Joel, Diana Peragine, Amy Muise, and Emily A. Impett, "Settling for Less Out of Fear of Being Single," *Journal of Personality and Social Psychology* 105, no. 6 (December 2013): 1049–73, https://www.ncbi.nlm.nih.gov/pubmed/24128187.

STEP THREE: STOP WASTING YOUR TIME

1. YouGov, *Relationship Book.*

2. YouGov, *Relationship Book.*

3. YouGov, *Relationship Book*.
4. YouGov, *Relationship Book*.
5. YouGov, *Relationship Book*.
6. YouGov, *Relationship Book*.
7. Zara Barrie, "Why True Love Isn't a Rapid Fire, It's a Slow Burn," Elite Daily, Bustle Digital Group, February 18, 2016, https://www.elite daily.com/dating/real-love-rapid-fire-slow-burn/1387847.

STEP FOUR: REFRAMING REJECTION

1. YouGov, *Relationship Book*.
2. Lauren C. Howe and Carol S. Dweck, "Changes in Self-Definition Impede Recovery from Rejection," *Personality and Social Psychology Bulletin* 42, no. 1 (October 23, 2015): 54–71, https://doi.org/10.1177/0146167215612743.
3. Clifton B. Parker, "Stanford Research Explains Why Some People Have More Difficulty Recovering from Romantic Breakups," *Stanford News*, Stanford University, January 7, 2016, https://news.stanford.edu/2016101/07/self-definition-breakups-010716/.
4. YouGov, *Relationship Book*.
5. YouGov, *Relationship Book*.

STEP FIVE: ACCEPTING THAT THE RIGHT PERSON LIKES YOU

1. YouGov, *Relationship Book*.
2. YouGov, *Relationship Book*.
3. Jodie Rogers, *The Stories We Tell Ourselves*, TEDxBerkleeValencia, 2014, https://www.youtube.com/watch?v=PXxBRhYseNY.
4. YouGov, *Relationship Book*.

STEP SIX: BE YOURSELF (NO, REALLY)

1. Candice Jalili, "Is Love at First Sight Even Real? Experts Say Probably Not," *Cosmopolitan*, April 24, 2019, https://www.cosmopolitan.com/sex-love/a27214571/loveatfirstsight/.
2. Lawrence Josephs, Benjamin Warach, Kirby L. Goldin, Peter K. Jonason, Bernard S. Gorman, Sanya Masroor, Nixza Lebron, "Be Yourself:

Authenticity as a Long-Term Mating Strategy," *Personality and Individual Differences* 143, no. 1 (June 2019): 118–127, https://doi.org/10.1016/j.paid.2019.02.020.

3. YouGov, *Relationship Book*.
4. YouGov, *Relationship Book*.
5. YouGov, *Relationship Book*.
6. YouGov, *Relationship Book*.
7. YouGov, *Relationship Book*.
8. YouGov, *Relationship Book*.
9. YouGov, *Relationship Book*.
10. YouGov, *Relationship Book*.
11. YouGov, *Relationship Book*.
12. YouGov, *Relationship Book*.

STEP SEVEN: THE BIG SEND

1. YouGov, *Relationship Book*.
2. YouGov, *Relationship Book*.
3. Candice Jalili, "Your Complete Guide to the DTR Talk," Swipe Life, Tinder, November 15, 2019, https:// swipelife.tinder.com/post/relationship-talk.
4. YouGov, *Relationship Book*.
5. YouGov, *Relationship Book*.
6. YouGov, *Relationship Book*.
7. "Singles in America," Match, 2019, https://singlesinamerica.com/.
8. YouGov, *Relationship Book*.
9. YouGov, *Relationship Book*.
10. YouGov, *Relationship Book*.
11. YouGov, *Relationship Book*.
12. YouGov, *Relationship Book*.
13. YouGov, *Relationship Book*.

BIBLIOGRAPHY

Alexandra, Rae. "Is 'The Bachelor' Franchise's Popularity Rooted in Fear of Social Progress?" KQED, August 9, 2018. https://www.kqed .org/pop/104953/is-the-bachelor-franchises-popularity-rooted-in -fear-of-social-progress.

"All the Single Ladies: 61% of Women in the UK Are Happy to Be Single, Compared to 49% of Men." Mintel, November 13, 2017. https://www .mintel.com/press-centre/social-and-lifestyle/all-the-single-ladies-61- of-women-in-the-uk-are-happy-to-be-single-compared-to-49-of-men.

Barrie, Zara. "Why True Love Isn't a Rapid Fire, It's a Slow Burn." Elite Daily, Bustle Digital Group, February 18, 2016. https://www.elitedaily .com/dating/real-love-rapid-fire-slow-burn/1387847.

Howe, Lauren C., and Carol S. Dweck. "Changes in Self-Definition Impede Recovery from Rejection." *Personality and Social Psychology Bulletin* 42, no. 1 (October 23, 2015): 54–71. https://doi.org/10.1177/0146167215612743.

Jalili, Candice. "Dating + Social Media: The New Rules." *Cosmopolitan*, May 2018, 109–13.

———. "DUI: Dating Under the Influence." *Cosmopolitan*, January 2018.

———. "Is Love at First Sight Even Real? Experts Say Probably Not." *Cosmopolitan*, April 24, 2019. https://www.cosmopolitan.com/sex -love/a27214571/loveatfirstsight/.

———. "7 Dating Pressures You Can Just Go Ahead and Ignore." Swipe Life, Tinder, July 24, 2019. https://swipelife.tinder.com/post/dating -stress.

———. "Your Complete Guide to the DTR Talk." Swipe Life, Tinder, November 15, 2019. https://swipelife.tinder.com/post/relationship-talk.

Josephs, Lawrence. "Why Authenticity Is the Best Dating Strategy." *Psychology Today*, March 2, 2019. https://www.psychologytoday.com/us/blog/between-the-sheets/201903/why-authenticity-is-the-best-dating-strategy.

Parker, Clifton B. "Stanford Research Explains Why Some People Have More Difficulty Recovering from Romantic Breakups." *Stanford News*, Stanford University, January 7, 2016. https://news.stanford.edu/20161/07/self-defintion-breakups-010716/.

Rosenfeld, Michael J., Reuben J. Thomas, and Sonia Hausen. "Disintermediating Your Friends: How Online Dating in the United States Displaces Other Ways of Meeting." *Proceedings of the National Academy of Sciences* 116, no. 36 (September 3, 2019): 17753–58. https://doi.org/10.1073/pnas.1908630116.

"Singles in America." Match, 2019. https://www.singlesinamerica.com/.

Spielmann, Stephanie S., Geoff MacDonald, Jessica A. Maxwell, Samantha Joel, Diana Peragine, Amy Muise, and Emily A. Impett. "Settling for Less Out of Fear of Being Single." *Journal of Personality and Social Psychology* 105, no. 6 (December 2013): 1049–73. https://www.ncbi.nlm.nih.gov/pubmed/24128187.

The Stories We Tell Ourselves. TEDxBerkleeValencia, 2014. https://www.youtube.com/watch?v=PXxBRhYseNY.

Wang, Wendy, and Kim Parker. "Record Share of Americans Have Never Married." Pew Research Center's Social & Demographic Trends Project. Pew Research Center, September 24, 2014. https://www.pewsocialtrends.org/2014/09/24/record-share-of-americans-have-never-married/.

YouGov on behalf of Candice Jalili. *Relationship Book*. March 13, 2020. Distributed by YouGov.

Candice Jalili was born in San Francisco and raised right across the Golden Gate in Marin County. After graduating from Santa Clara University, she decided to move to New York to work for Elite Daily, where she currently holds the title of Senior Sex + Dating Writer. Candice's musings on relationships can also regularly be found in *Cosmopolitan*, on Tinder Swipe Life and The Cut, in *Time*, and more. She covers pretty much every topic you and your friends discuss over boozy brunch—from why you're still thinking about your ex to the latest celebrity hookup. She's also really, really, *really* over smart, cool women sacrificing their own sanity in an attempt to "get the guy."